The Survival of Images

Kritik: German Literary Theory and Cultural Studies

LILIANE WEISSBERG, EDITOR

*A complete listing of the books in this series can be found
at the back of this volume.*

The Survival of Images

Art Historians, Psychoanalysts, and the Ancients

Louis Rose

WAYNE STATE UNIVERSITY PRESS   DETROIT

05   04   03   02   01   1   2   3   4   5

Library of Congress Cataloging-in-Publication Data

Rose, Louis.
The survival of images : art historians, psychoanalysts, and the ancients / Louis Rose.
p. cm.—(Kritik, german literary theory and cultural studies)
Includes bibliographical references and index.
ISBN 0-8143-2860-1 ISBN 0-8143-2861-x (pbk.)
1. Psychology—History—20th century. 2. Psychoanalysis and
culture—History—20th century. 3. Art, Modern—20th century—History.
I. Title. II. Kritik (Detroit, Mich.)
BF105 .R67 2001
111'.85'09041—dc21   2001002874

FOR CINDY

Contents

ILLUSTRATIONS

Acknowledgments

The director of Wayne State University Press, Arthur B. Evans, supported the book manuscript from its earliest phase of writing. The project editor, Adela Garcia, patiently read the manuscript and guided it through the publication process. My thanks also extend to Tammy Oberhausen Rastoder for copyediting the final draft.

Otterbein College granted a sabbatical leave allowing for completion of the book. The college's Ursula Holtermann Fund assisted with completion of the project. From the Otterbein College library, Jessica Mize, Allen Reichert, and Patricia Rothermich generously located necessary sources.

I wish to express my appreciation to Professor Sir Ernst Gombrich for his response to an inquiry regarding Ernst Kris.

Finally, for their commentary and advice on the manuscript I once more owe a deep debt of gratitude to Jim Amelang and Liliane Weissberg.

The first who likened painting and poetry to each other must
have been a man of delicate perception,
who found that both arts affected him in a similar manner.
Both, he realised, present to us appearance as reality,
absent things as present; both deceive,
and the deceit of either is pleasing.

GOTTHOLD EPHRAIM LESSING
Laocoon or On the Limits of Painting and Poetry
1766

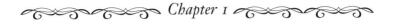

Image-making and Movement

I

In 1895, the year in which Sigmund Freud began to interpret dreams, Louis Lumière completed the invention of the motion picture camera. With his new mechanical creation Lumière originated a cultural industry, initiating an age of moving images. Cranked by hand rather than powered by electricity, and designed to be transportable, the new apparatus allowed Lumière, in the manner of an Impressionist painter, to leave the studio with his tools and to record a world in movement. According to Erik Barnouw, the French inventor conceived his camera as "an ideal instrument for catching life on the run—'sur le vif,' as Lumière put it."[1] In 1893, only two years before the filmmaker introduced his invention to the public, the young art historian Aby Warburg published his dissertation on Botticelli in which he examined the use of accessories of motion in Renaissance painting. Warburg's theme reminds us that artists working with marble or pigment had been the first to give to their images a sense of living movement, an artistic tradition which possibly had reached Lumière through his father, Antoine Lumière, who worked as both a painter and photographer.[2]

The influence which painting exerted on moving pictures revealed itself perhaps most strikingly in the films of a director such as Jean Renoir, the son of the Impressionist Pierre Auguste Renoir. Single frames from

Renoir's movies can be isolated and appreciated as scenes possessing their own life, yet the autonomous quality of such scenes does not detract from the natural development or storytelling of the film as a whole. Other directors have not so easily repeated Renoir's achievement, which derived in great part from his sense of the living presence which could be conveyed within a single image, whether an image composed on canvas or on film.[3]

Beyond transferring techniques of painting from the canvas to the reel of film, Renoir sought to transform the motion picture into a new stage for theater. In an interview toward the end of his career he described his approach to film directing: "I work with the actors. I want to have an idea of my scene due to the rehearsal. When I have a clear idea of my scene, all of a sudden I realize everything I was doing was wrong. I start again. Finally, when the scene shows something which seems to me sufficient, I bring the camera."[4] Movie frames originated as the traces of a stage action. Having gained new existence on camera such traces acquired further life from the efforts of the audience. For Renoir the movie itself represented a fragment which the spectator had to complete: "You know what is my preoccupation in pictures? When the picture is finished? It is that I would like the picture to give the feeling to the audience that i[t] is unfinished. Because, I believe that the work of art where the spectator, where the reviewer, does not collaborate is not a work of art. I like the people who look at the picture, perhaps, to build a different story on the side."[5] Thus with Renoir the new art of motion pictures relied on the achievements not only of the visual arts but also of the theater: the re-creation of an action, the construction of a scene, the encounter of stage and spectator. That dramaturgic approach to filmmaking and to the audience may in fact have reflected a lesson learned from his revolutionary painter-father, who cautioned his son in the following words: "To express himself well, the artist should be hidden. Take the actors of ancient Greece with their masks, for example."[6] With the camera the son translated onto film the qualities of movement and expression which derived from the masked enactments of the original amphitheater, his success as a dramatist, as well as an image-maker perhaps most clearly evident in the final frames of *Grand Illusion*, in which the French prisoners of war, Maréchal and Rosenthal advanced with arduous and deliberate motions toward an invisible Swiss border, seeking a place of refuge and an end to their journey of return.

Through the medium of film Jean Renoir not only captured images on the run but linked them to a dramatic pattern. In the first decades of the twentieth century Aby Warburg and Sigmund Freud applied a similar approach within the sphere of cultural science. Concerning themselves with the problem of how artistic or mental images produced the illusion of living movement—or to borrow the language of film, with how they became moving pictures—the art historian and the psychoanalyst concluded that such images came to life as visual and emotional fragments of a drama. As cultural scientists Warburg and Freud sought to connect the sense of living movement within individual artistic products to patterns of thought and behavior which appeared within the amphitheater.

At the turn of the century cultural investigators who included classicists and anthropologists, literary critics and social theorists explored links between the singular creations of artists and the collective products of culture such as myth, ritual, and theater. In such links they sought fundamental principles of both the creative process and cultural change. Art historians and psychologists made increasingly significant contributions to that search. As Jacob Burckhardt confidently claimed, the products of art preserved visible traces not only of the lives of artists but also of the consciousness or spirit of their times. For its part the new science of psychology offered principles of cognition and motivation, principles which operated across both time and place, providing the basis for universal laws of artistic invention and cultural change. Karl Lamprecht, whose lectures on art and cultural history Aby Warburg attended at the University of Bonn, constructed from his own psychological interpretation of artwork both a new research method and a new theory of historical stages, on account of which he fell victim to the polemical fury of far more traditional German historians. In the first half of the twentieth century, however, art historical studies and psychological investigations gave vital impetus to the growth and transformation of cultural research.[7]

This book examines a small circle of art historians and psychoanalysts as cultural scientists. Specifically, it focuses on a group of investigators whose careers followed different paths, yet who demonstrated important connections to each other, both direct and indirect: Aby Warburg (1866–1929), art historian and founder of the Warburg Library of Cultural Science (*Kulturwissenschaftliche Bibliothek Warburg*); Sigmund Freud (1856–1939), creator of psychoanalysis; Emanuel Loewy (1857–1938), leading classicist at the universities in Vienna and Rome, and a friend of Freud; Fritz Saxl (1890–1948), Warburg's successor; and Ernst Kris (1900–1957), Viennese art historian-turned-psychoanalyst. These interpreters of art and the psyche explored not only how images reflected creative processes and cultural transformations, but also how they visually and psychologically preserved the remnants of enactments and dramatizations from the past. Such residues persisted within images of movement and became revived or redramatized through contact with the present. In the following chapters the term *mimesis* will refer to the survival and regeneration of those dramatic fragments.

Freud and Warburg shared not only a bond as cultural researchers but also a link, if less directly, through the city of Vienna. Aby Warburg's own life and career oscillated between two cities: his native Hamburg and his adopted home of Florence. Hamburg eventually became the site of his Library of Cultural Science. Still, although Warburg never resided in Vienna, his legacy became significantly joined to the work and fate of the Viennese. The young Viennese scholar, Fritz Saxl, became Warburg's assistant at the library in Hamburg on the eve of the First World War and later followed as its director. Saxl engineered the library's expansion into a research institute, its cooperation with the University of Hamburg, and its safe transfer to England after the Nazi seizure of power, remaining as its director throughout the Second World War. Ernst Kris, the leading interpreter of art among the second generation of Viennese psychoanalysts, participated in projects organized by Saxl, and himself combined Freudian psychology, Warburgian method, and ancient studies in his own early writings on the artist. Furthermore, he recommended his art historical colleagues, Otto Kurz and E. H. Gombrich as assistants to Saxl in London. Both Kurz and Gombrich remained with the Warburg Institute throughout their careers, Kurz serving as its librarian and Gombrich becoming its director in 1959. Ancient studies in Vienna had helped to prepare Kris for both Freudian and Warburgian researches: his professor in ancient history at the University of Vienna, Emanuel Loewy had employed his own psychological theory of memory to explain both artistic creation in archaic Greece and the trend toward the imitation of nature in classical artwork. The researches of Warburg, Freud, and Loewy revealed a common concern with the question of dramatic survivals, or mimesis—a concern which their Viennese successors Kris and Saxl preserved, expanded, and reformulated after the First World War.

II

In the case of Warburg, Freud, and their successors, interest in the connection between images and drama sustained the classical tradition of criticism as transmitted by the work of G. E. Lessing. In antiquity Aristotle had emphasized that drama, in contrast to painting and sculpture, generated a sense of living movement by representing an action in the form of an action. Pursuing the philosopher's insight, Lessing in his *Laocoon* treatise, defined the illusion of movement as the essential dilemma of both poetry and painting, neither of whose crafts could call upon "the living artistry of the actor."[8] By its very nature, painting had to confine itself to representing fragments of motion, yet through such fragments indicate the dramatic framework to which they attached: "Painting, in her co-existing compositions, can use only one single moment of the action, and must therefore choose the most pregnant, from which what precedes and follows will be most easily apprehended."[9] Because visual artists—sculptors as well as painters—remained necessarily confined to presenting a single moment, they had to resist the impulse to depict in that one instant the whole emotional force which properly belonged only to the entire dramatic action. Thus, unconstrained movement or excessive gesturing proved inappropriate, even destructive to the visual arts. Painting approached its limits when seeking to represent the quality of grace, that quality which Lessing defined as "beauty in motion."[10] The Enlightenment critic passed severe judgment. The painter who endeavored to convey graceful movement "can only help us to guess the motion, but in fact his figures are motionless.

Consequently grace with him is turned into grimace."[11] Ernst Kris perhaps followed a clue from Lessing: the psychoanalyst sought the principles of artistic creativity not in gracious but rather in grimacing figures, in whose distorted features he nonetheless discovered an impulse to motion which illuminated the contrary achievement of grace.

The link between Warburgian and Freudian scholars thus included an intellectual influence traceable to Lessing, an influence which reached not only Warburg but also Freud through the city of Hamburg. Freud's wife, Martha Bernays, belonged to the Hamburg Bernays family. Her grandfather, Isaak Bernays, who in 1821 was appointed chief rabbi of the city's Jewish community, had built cooperation in political and charitable aims between Hamburg's traditional Orthodox synagogue and the city's newly created Reform congregation. In the year Isaak Bernays became Hamburg's chief rabbi the legal emancipation of the Jewish community had yet to occur—it finally came in 1860—but the city's classical academy began in 1802 to accept Jewish students. There the chief rabbi enrolled his son—Martha Bernays's uncle—Jacob Bernays, the future classical philologist.[12] In a well-known letter written in 1882 to his fiancée in Hamburg, the young Freud identified Rabbi Isaak Bernays with the figure of Nathan, the Jewish patriarch who combined Enlightenment rationalism and toleration with traditional religious sagacity and loyalty in Lessing's play, *Nathan the Wise*. Referring to the chief rabbi's own enlightened approach, Freud wrote that in Isaak Bernays's

> method of teaching lay enormous progress, a kind of education of mankind in Lessing's sense. Religion was no longer treated as a rigid dogma, it became an object of reflection for the satisfaction of cultivated artistic taste and of intensified logical efforts, and the teacher of Hamburg recommended it finally not because it happened to exist and had been declared holy, but because he was pleased by the deeper meaning which he found in it or which he projected into it.[13]

Rather than a traditional rabbinic figure, Isaak Bernays represented a successor to Lessing, teaching religion as he would art and philosophy—as a sublime human creation. Freud, who early in life left the path of religious tradition, applied in his own work the method which he originally associated with Lessing's Hamburg representative: to interpret religion by locating from an emotional and intellectual distance the mental projections which produced it. The future psychoanalyst adopted the vantage point of a spectator within the amphitheater contemplating the stage action before him.

In his later psychological work Freud recalled a second message from Lessing's Nathan: that traditional attitudes and bonds reasserted themselves even—or perhaps especially—among supposedly emancipated minds. Such psychological survivals tended to reappear in instances of Freud's own ritualistic behavior, for example in his repeated visits in Rome to Michelangelo's sculpture of Moses, in whose presence Freud felt both religious rebelliousness and a sense of personal identification.[14] In *Jokes and their Relation to the Unconscious*, Freud perhaps referred specifically to himself when he quoted from *Nathan the Wise*, "Not all are free who mock their chains."[15]

Aby Warburg demonstrated far greater apostasy than did Freud, but not without vestiges of conflict which surfaced on significant ritual occasions. As Felix Gilbert pointed out, among the most prominent Jewish banking families in Imperial Germany the Warburg family stood alone for having rejected the path of official religious conversion.[16] Aby Warburg, however, ultimately withdrew from Hamburg's Jewish Community organization, in which his father had come to play a leading part, and pursued his chief cultural role as private scholar within Germany's higher academic circles. Upon his father's death in 1910, Warburg's inward struggles concerning his religious past resurfaced, struggles which he recorded in his diary. Jewish tradition required that Warburg, as the eldest son, recite kaddish, the prayer of remembrance, at a memorial service to be held in his father's synagogue. In his journal he wrote that "I am to take part in a mourning service requiring my active participation in the cult, thereby putting in these circumstances a clan-like seal on the moral inheritance of the members of the family. There is no style in this, especially if one respects Father. My respect for him lies in my not hushing up the absolute antithesis in *Weltanschauung* through an external cultic act: for I am dissident."[17] The son escaped his dilemma by declining attendance at the service. In his art historical work, however, Warburg by that time had already begun to explore ancient ritual survivals in modern cultural life—chiefly the life of the Florentine Renaissance patriciate, with whom he claimed an inward identification.[18]

Even more prominently than in the case of Freud, Lessing's work helped to guide Warburg's early intellectual pursuits. Fritz Saxl became the first biographer of Warburg to trace the art historian's interest in early Renaissance painting to the influence of the German Enlightenment critic, who had himself resided in Warburg's native city while director of the short-lived National Theater. Saxl explained: "The study of Lessing's *Laocoon* had roused his interest in the arts. Lessing had lived in Hamburg, and there was in Warburg's school a local tradition for the study of eighteenth-century art criticism. Lessing's thesis is well known. The artist and the poet are subject to different rules. Whereas the sculptor is not allowed to represent Laocoon screaming, the poet has a right to give unrestrained expression to his hero's sufferings"[19] (Figure 1). Yet, Saxl continued, Warburg "saw that Botticelli and his contemporaries had not been primarily interested in the quiet dignity of classical marbles like Lessing's contemporaries, but had borrowed from both sculptors and poets the very means of representing exaggerated movement."[20] While Warburg followed Lessing in focusing on how images of movement transmitted fragments of dramatic events, he departed from Lessing's example by finding in such images a primordial emotional lineage which linked pagan dramaturgy to Renaissance gestures, and more broadly, ancient culture to modern life.

An exemplar of classical learning, Lessing not only embodied an ideal of critical distance to which both Freud and Warburg subscribed but also identified the object of cultural study common to the psychoanalyst and art historian: the image of movement. Both researchers regarded the eighteenth-century writer as that intellectual figure who conveyed the humanist tradition of interpretation to their own worlds of experience and scholarship—either through the Bernays family or the academic circles of Hamburg. Ernst Cassirer, one of the first Hamburg university professors to participate in the projects of the Warburg Library, found in Lessing a similar model. In Cassirer's view, Lessing pioneered " 'productive' criticism,"[21] an aesthetic analysis which entered into the creative process itself. That form of criticism approached artistic tradition from a motive "which

1. *Laocoon*. Vatican Museums. Photo: Alinari/Art Resource, New York.

does not spring from any opposition to the prevailing order but which feels within itself the power and the impulse to transform things so that they will not become entrenched in rigidity."[22] Criticism demanded distance, but itself became an agent of renewal, a participant in the creative transformation of classicism. Indeed, Elizabeth Butler—among the first British scholars to publish in the Warburg Library's London journal—argued that Lessing the critic conceived of himself as the protagonist of a drama, and that his analysis of the Laocoon sculpture represented a theatrical performance in prose. That combative and dignified essay conjured in imagination a stage scene occupied continuously by the Laocoon group, before which Lessing confronted successive antagonists drawn from the world of criticism.[23] As an essayist Lessing thus enacted the roles of both actor and spectator, creator and observer. Edgar Wind, an early and active member of the library's Hamburg circle, recalled that Warburg similarly perceived criticism as the opportunity not only for reflection but also for the revival of absent images: "Warburg was convinced that in his own work, when he was reflecting upon the images he analysed, he was fulfilling an analogous function to that of pictorial memory when, under the compulsive urge to expression, the mind spontaneously synthesizes images, namely the recollection of pre-existing forms."[24] For Warburg, art history—as Lessing demonstrated—continually pressed beyond static critical confines to seek a dynamic, unbounded stage.

Finally, Lessing's own work as a playwright perhaps exerted an influence on Freud and Warburg equal to that of his critical labors. In tracing visual images to their roots in the primordial past, Freud and Warburg reinterpreted and reapplied the universalism with which the dramatist concluded *Nathan the Wise*, whose Jewish, Christian, and Muslim characters ultimately became aware that an actual family bond existed between them, the bond not of blood relation, but of clan identity. As cultural researchers, Freud and Warburg unearthed within classical culture the surviving fragments of a primitive clan tradition—even, according to Freud, the traces of a primal family horde. The universalism within classical culture possessed roots in primordial clan behavior. Such a perspective on antiquity perhaps seemed fitting. From the time of Aeschylus ancient drama itself demanded the recognition of a hidden clan mechanism within civilization.[25]

III

The following book might best be described as an extended essay. It delineates an intellectual perspective, or angle of vision, from which to explore the work of both art historians and psychoanalysts. Its approach represents a continuation of the author's previous publication in the *Kritik* series which discussed early Viennese psychoanalysis as a movement to transform the cultural sciences.[26] By emphasizing certain common features in the work of Sigmund Freud and Aby Warburg—and in the work of their immediate successors—the current essay widens that focus to examine how Freudianism in Vienna and the early Warburg school contributed jointly to redefining the field of cultural research. Recently, several studies of Aby Warburg's scholarship have noted parallels between Warburg's vision and that of Freud: their concern with the problem of interpretive distance, their attention to cultural and artistic details as outcroppings of memory, and their fatalism toward the psychological demands of civilization.[27] The following study pursues a systematic comparison of ideas which the author hopes will provide a further contribution not only to students of the Warburgian school of art history, but also to researchers in the areas of Freudian theory and European intellectual history. The comparison will explore how both Warburg and Freud evolved dramaturgic approaches to cultural science.

Still, while this study will illuminate features which art history and psychoanalysis held in common, it does not intend thereby to blur or diminish significant distinctions which existed between the two disciplines—or between the writings of the specific individuals under study. Fritz Saxl did not apply psychological analysis to individual works of art, stating in fact that it was "always dangerous to look at pictures with an eye on the painter's psychology."[28] Yet, when confronting for example the medieval revival of pagan astrology, Saxl as a cultural investigator demonstrated a concern with "the psychology of such a change of mental climate,"[29] or an interest in what he termed "historical psychology."[30] Furthermore, he included a psychological element within his description of European humanism, a program which he defined as "all endeavour to express our feelings where they touch the very roots of our being in accordance with the spirit of the classics."[31] Though not pursuing a psychology of art, Saxl recognized that art history posed questions of direct interest to the mental scientist.

In 1921, in a letter to his friend and colleague, Ludwig Binswanger, Freud expressed not only his hope for Aby Warburg's recovery at Binswanger's Kreuzlingen psychiatric clinic but also his interest in Warburg's "clear-sighted works."[32] Freud never referred in his own publications to the art historian's findings; further, for his part Warburg firmly opposed Freudian sexual theory.[33] Still, both the psychoanalyst and the art historian placed image-making at the center of their researches, exploring how visual pictures and scenes gained qualities of immediacy and living movement. According to both, those qualities of pictures and performances resulted from dramatic fragments of the past coming into renewed contact with the present. The medium of that contact or exchange remained Europe's classical inheritance, that legacy which transmitted both ancient enlightenment and primeval paganism. Projections of primal emotions and traces of primordial expressive action survived within transcendent classical motions reproduced on canvas, in stone, or on stage. Image-making in the classical tradition thus provided a means of return, drawing the ancient into a dynamic and disquieting relationship with the modern—a relationship which Warburg described as "the afterlife of antiquity."[34]

In tracing the origins and significance of images, Freudian and Warburgian researchers examined closely the disruptive influence of survivals, and the impact of mimetic activity on the ego, specifically on the identities of the artist, actor, and spectator. In ritual performance Warburg perceived the threat of a loss of self, a danger which resurfaced for the artist who revived pagan images. As Horst Bredekamp wrote, both Freud and Warburg concerned themselves with the persistence of primal projective mechanisms: "For Freud, like Warburg, the individual faces daily the task of distancing, of freeing oneself from blindly projecting one's own instinctive motives onto the surroundings and thereby in a magical or neurotic way confusing the ego with the world."[35] For Kris, image-making revealed the vital and uncertain nature of the ego's contact and communication with the world. Searching within images for clues as to how the artist revived traces of the past, Saxl also developed an interest in how the artist defined through his work his own shifting engagement with the world of his contemporaries.

In his own day Saxl observed a rapidly expanding influence for the activity of image-making, and for the study of images. Characterizing the twentieth century from a cultural viewpoint he wrote that "this age of ours is not an age of reason, but a visual age, and many of us are more inclined to draw enlightenment and intellectual pleasure and exultation from images than from the printed or the spoken word."[36] Classicism had begun to merge with modern visual culture, opening a new avenue for researching the afterlife of antiquity. While Freud and Warburg explored the classical tradition by tracking its origins to clan ceremonies and primal ritual, Saxl ultimately followed the ancient tradition forward, charting its transformation and renewal within the modernist art of Paul Cézanne.

The following essay will thus keep distinctions in view. It will, however, chiefly stress parallel endeavors, and in that way indicate the degree to which both art history and psychoanalysis developed in the first half of the twentieth century as comparable schools of thought. Those schools twice renewed themselves: first, during the brief recovery which followed the First World War, and second, during the years of exile from the European continent which began with the rise of Nazism in Germany and Austria, and which continued into the period of reconstruction after the Second World War.

IV

The problem of creating the illusion of movement confronted not only the visual arts, but also, as Lessing indicated, the field of literature. Indeed, the success of literary realism depended in crucial part upon an effective imagery of motion. In his masterwork, *Mimesis: The Representation of Reality in Western Literature*, Erich Auerbach identified two ancient models for conveying the sense of living movement through literature: the Homeric epic and the Jewish Biblical tradition. In the *Iliad* and *Odyssey*, Homer depicted the world through its external forms: the entire content of the poems became in Homeric language immediately open to the senses. What human beings in the poems, or in life, did not directly observe—the inward motives of others—the poet's characters explicated in speeches. Humanity became fully knowable only in actions, whether acts of speech or observable deeds. To represent human reality the Homeric tradition therefore isolated moments of such action. The Biblical literary tradition, on the other hand, conceived of living reality as a truth or purpose imbedded within history. That truth could not be isolated and observed: it remained hidden, although it made its presence felt in historical events. Those events, therefore, demanded interpretation and inspired remembrance.[37]

In the two types of imagery—representation of an outward action and allusion to an internal moving principle—one recognizes not only different techniques of generating a sense of movement but also two separate understandings of the past and of art. Both perspectives emerged in the work of the psychoanalysts and art historians under consideration. Aby Warburg, for example, applied the term *pathos formula* to describe an image of motion that conveyed the impulse to an action, or the feeling which accompanied that action. At the same time, however, Warburg's term implied the preservation of an external remnant of that act. Similarly, Sigmund Freud considered images in the visual arts, like dream pictures, to be disguised embodiments of unconscious drives: the meaning of an image derived from its inward motive force. Image-making thus provided a model of sublimation, that psychical process by which repressed libidinal wishes became channeled into nonsexual, cultural aims. Yet, after he turned his attention to ritual behavior Freud also began to search in art for the survivals of historical deeds and events.

In discussing techniques of realism, Auerbach identified a literary approach distinct from the ancient focus on either external deeds or invisible truths. That approach sought to represent the changing and problematic relation between the ego and the modern world. In Stendhal's novels

Auerbach found expressed the uneasy relationship between the self and society in a Europe transformed by the French Revolution, a revolution which subjected the very nature of experience to a new swiftness and wide-reaching quality of events:

> Such a development abrogates or renders powerless the entire social structure of orders and categories previously held valid; the tempo of the changes demands a perpetual and extremely difficult effort toward inner adaptation and produces intense concomitant crises. He who would account to himself for his real life and his place in human society is obliged to do so upon a far wider practical foundation and in a far larger context than before, and to be continually conscious that the social base upon which he lives is not constant for a moment but is perpetually changing through convulsions of the most various kinds.[38]

Stendhal himself never found a stable connection to the new society: as Auerbach emphasized, "he always feels and experiences the reality of his period as a resistance."[39] The sense of living movement and immediacy which Stendhal imparted to his writings reflected, therefore, "his fight for self-assertion."[40] The modern technique of literary realism thus derived from an ego activity, from what Kris described as the striving for an autonomous, integrated self in opposition to the protean quality of external reality. The image of movement not only isolated a moment of action or embodied an inward impulse but represented the ego's struggle to endure the world.

V

In the true spirit of the classical inheritance Lessing argued that "we can generally recall a movement more easily and more vividly than mere forms and colours."[41] Following in Lessing's tradition, Aby Warburg and Sigmund Freud conceived of the image of movement as a type of remembrance. Whereas Warburg spoke of the afterlife of antiquity, Freud referred to the return of the repressed. Both researchers explored images of motion for survivals of the past. Although Emanuel Loewy investigated archaic artworks that renounced the depiction of movement, he too explained artistic creativity as a form of recollection. Like the ancients, the art historians and psychologists under discussion recognized in Mnemosyne the mother of the Muses.

By conceiving of image-making as an art of remembrance, psychoanalysts and art historians confronted the manufacturing of images as a means through which persons created comprehensible and adaptive links between the past and present. For Warburg, the construction of images provided an opportunity for organizing fragments of the past, and therefore promised the self a greater sense of control: art thus preserved an uneasy affinity with magical beliefs and practices, while preparing the ground for the triumph of rationalism. In a different, but not unrelated context, Kris concluded that image-making, whether in the act of play or the course of conscious artistic endeavor, derived from an effort at integrating past and present experiences. Through the ego's synthetic function images again maintained an afterlife, but a life which acquired new significance within the changing conditions of an individual's or society's history.

Images gained meaning not only as revenants of the past but also as creations by audiences in the present. With Warburg and Freud, the Aristotelian approach remained influential: encountering a work of art, the observer experienced a catharsis, a release of emotions. The successors of Warburg and Freud particularly emphasized, however, the active role of the spectator in giving new meaning to aesthetic images. Kris examined how audiences inwardly reinvented artistic images, or reexperienced their very creation, a process not dissimilar to that which Saxl explored from an art historical point of view in the Venetian reception of classical artworks. For both Freudian and Warburgian interpreters of art, such communication between artists and spectators formed one of the inherent phases of image-making itself.

The idea of image-making as an endeavor shared by artist and audience applied to an understanding not only of the visual arts but also of religion and ritual behavior. Specifically, ceremonial performances demanded the mutual sympathy and equal participation of actor and spectator: both sets of participants re-created primal emotional attitudes and historical roles, and in that regard belonged to a common circle of initiates. Rites of initiation—ancient sources perhaps of theatrical performances—combined introduction into a new community or new state of existence with the revival of fragments from the past. Beyond the joining of artist and audience such ceremonial rites served to represent an idealized version—or prototype—of behavior: initiates did not embark upon a new phase of existence without experiencing an archetypal portion of the past. Locating prototypical images, unearthing their primal origins, and charting their transformations belonged, according to Freud, Warburg, and Loewy, to the preeminent tasks of cultural science.

Remembrance, unification of artist and audience, and idealization defined cultural functions which image-making shared with ritual enactment. Those functions belonged also to the process of psychological identification. As Freud and later psychoanalysts emphasized, individuals constructed their identities from a combination of diverse motives, among them the desire to remember, the urge to copy, and the striving after ideals. As Freud also stressed, the process of identification became laced with ambivalence. The act of identifying sought to restore a lost object—in Lessing's words, to produce "absent things as present"[42]—and thus represented an act of recovery in the sense of both remembering and healing. By incorporating the absent object as an ideal the ego not only performed a gesture of attachment but also constructed an internal model for engagement with the world. Through imitation the ego experimented with that model, simultaneously reviving portions of a previous state and generating a new presence. Yet, to imitate meant also to replace, an act which satisfied rebellious or hostile impulses. Such aggression could turn inward: through the activity of imitation the self abandoned its own identity. Having sacrificed both itself and its attachment to external objects, the ego remained condemned to a world of its own projections.

The conflicting meanings of identification recalled the origins of dramatic performance in the classical amphitheater. As Jean-Pierre Vernant explained, the Greek dramatist transformed the exemplary, idealized image of the epic hero into a struggling, enigmatic figure: "But within the space of the stage and the framework of tragic representation, the hero is no longer put forward as a model, as he used to be in epic and in lyric poetry. Now he has become a problem."[43] The tragic poet not only transformed the figure of hero but metamorphosed the artist himself from narrator into imitator, redesigning the tragic stage as an arena for his own imitative fiction. Thus Vernant further contrasted the epic storyteller to the tragic artist: "What the public sees before it in the theater is not a poet recounting the trials withstood in ancient times by men now gone whose absence is, so to speak, implied by the very narration. Instead, those trials take place before its very eyes, adopting the form of real existence in the immediacy of the performance. The tragic poet becomes totally invisible behind the characters on stage, acting and speaking for themselves as if alive."[44] The tragedian unceremoniously withdrew from the performance so as to allow the reappearance of figures from the legendary past: Vernant emphasized that the "precise meaning of *mimeisthai*, to imitate, is to simulate the presence of one who is absent."[45] The reenactment of the legendary hero's sufferings on the tragic stage removed his story from a chronological narrative of events, and placed it within a universal and necessary pattern of human destiny.

The shift from narrative to imitation, from the epic mode to the tragic marked the crucial transition from a ritualistic to a dramatic worldview. Toward the end of the archaic period recitations which recounted the speeches and actions of gods and heroes became joined to religious festivals, a foreshadowing of the birth of classical tragic enactments.[46] When the poet ceased the practice of reciting such speech and action but turned instead to imitating, or re-creating, them through dialogue and motion, dramatic presentation began to take shape. As Vernant explained, in the tragic age "the act of *mimeisthai* was a performance, a demonstration."[47] Mimesis led spectators to perceive the actor as a figure other than his own self. Through the skill of miming and the use of the mask, the performer created an identity between himself and the other, the absent one. Tragic dramaturgy, as Vernant described, demanded "identification: *mimēsis* implies that, by adopting the other's ways, the simulator becomes just like the one he is intending to mimic."[48] Classical sculptors and painters, working from marble blocks and vivid pigments, in one regard amplified that stage vision by infusing images of absent objects with a revolutionary sense of movement. Such also was the dramatic vision of Freud, who perceived in the figure of the suffering tragic hero a revival of the absent primal patriarch, the original model of identification.

VI

At the turn of the twentieth century classical scholars investigated the problem of cultural transmission by exploring the persistence of ritual elements within tragic performances. To what extent did ritual enactments survive within ancient drama? Friedrich Nietzsche proclaimed that the classical dramatic vision preserved the essential core of primal rites: the Dionysian sacrifice of self-consciousness in an effort to achieve identification with the suffering god. The tragic chorus embodied the circle of fervent Dionysian celebrants who submerged themselves in the ritual enactment of the life, death, and rebirth of the deity. Tragedy generated impassioned reenactments on stage and visceral responses within the audience but directed actors and spectators toward the ultimate achievement of Apollonian self-awareness and intellectual lucidity. For Warburg—who reflected the influence of Nietzsche as well as Lessing—the ritual sacrifice of the ego remained a primordial survival not only within tragedy but also within painting and sculpture. Against that legacy, the Apollonian goal of art sought the recovery of the self.[49]

Nietzschean interest in ritual survivals extended from classical scholarship on the continent to ancient studies in Britain, where both the Warburgian and Freudian schools found refuge between the wars. England at the turn of the century produced a circle of classicists known widely as the Cambridge ritualists. The circle's founding members—Jane Ellen Harrison, Gilbert Murray, and Francis M. Cornford—belonged among the twentieth-century pathfinders in ancient scholarship and archaeology. Harrison, Murray, and Cornford agreed that the revolutionary triumphs of Greek art, drama, and philosophy not only had their origins in primitive Greek ritual and religion but that primal customs and impulses survived within even the highest achievements of the Classical Age. To recognize those primitive survivals classicists had to familiarize themselves with the most recent advances in anthropology and psychology, including the new ideas of Freud. The original Cambridge ritualists not only reenvisioned the influence of the primitive past on antiquity but introduced new psychological and anthropological methods of working to the field of ancient studies: in their view, classical scholarship had to become a cultural science.[50]

The early Cambridge school traced the sources of classical drama and art to rituals which supplicated and propitiated that force which governed earthly transitions between life, death, and rebirth—in the Greek world, a force embodied in the god Dionysos. In her book, *Ancient Art and Ritual*, Jane Ellen Harrison charted the transformation of ceremonial rites into dramatic performances, and finally into sculptural creations. According to Harrison, ritual enactments produced imitations of deeds—either remembered or anticipated—with the aim of awakening and expressing vital emotions. Mimesis, or dramatic enactment, referred not to the simple act of copying but recalled the effort by a primitive dancer or celebrant "to emphasize, enlarge, enhance, his own personality; he masquerades, he does not mimic."[51] Ancient drama employed elements of primitive performances, but only after having created "Psychical Distance."[52] The dramatic act of imitating the god or hero allowed emotional expression, but individuals did not expect the stage act, unlike the ritual enactment, to exert direct influence on the physical or spiritual realms. The effect of tragedy operated only at a distance—the distance at which imitation emerged as drama. Celebrants became spectators, who sat outside the performing circle in an audience area, or "theater," and performers behaved as actors, who, when not delivering their parts, removed themselves to an offstage space, or "scene." Sculpture completed the process of distancing, a process embodied in the statue of the Apollo Belvedere, whose gesturing indicated "not a dance, but a flight"[53] (Figure 2). Yet, sculptures did not entirely escape their ritual backgrounds, because within them the observer might still detect "rites caught and fixed and frozen."[54] As Harrison concluded, "art *arises from* ritual, and ritual is in its essence a faded action, an imitation."[55] In the contemporary world, the image of movement— or fragment of drama—preserved what remained of that ritual act, and

2. *Apollo Belvedere*. Vatican Museums. Photo: Alinari/Art Resource, New York.

transmitted its primordial emotive influence. The effect of mimesis thus drew upon primal, ceremonial origins.

It is difficult in this book to join under a single name psychoanalysts and art historians who belonged to different generations, who saw their professional careers in differing lights, and who harbored crucial interpretive disagreements. To a limited extent it would not be inappropriate to borrow the designation used for the Cambridge circle and refer to those psychologists and art scholars as ritualists. Such a name applies not only to their interest in the emotional and visual afterlife of the primal past in classical, humanist culture but also to their effort at shaping a cultural science which would interpret that afterlife. Further, the description calls to mind that at the beginning of the century there already existed an intellectual link between the cultural sciences on the continent and in Britain.

Yet, while the term *ritualist* serves a certain purpose, it does not indicate the extent to which Warburg and Freud—the twentieth-century followers of Lessing—continued to view cultural processes as if unfolding within the circle of the amphitheater. The ancients who had acted upon the stage or had observed the masked performances below them envisaged history itself within a dramaturgic schema.[56] Adhering to that classical vision Lessing had defined the essential question confronting the artist. By what means did a single fragment or image convey a drama? According to Warburg and Freud, that same question confronted the modern cultural scientist. In exploring the afterlife of pagan antiquity the art historian and the psychoanalyst traced how absent objects reappeared on new stages and behind new masks, their movements governed by a primordial tragic necessity.

In examining the contributions of Warburgian art historians and Freudian psychologists to the development of a new branch of cultural research, this book begins with the decade of European intellectual ferment preceding the First World War and concludes with the years immediately following the Second World War—a time period during which cultural contacts throughout continental Europe survived almost solely in exile. Thus our study begins with the cities of Hamburg and Florence, moves to Vienna, and reaches its conclusion in London. England ultimately became the new home—or the first step toward such a home—for art historians and psychoanalysts seeking refuge from Germany and Austria, researchers from the continent who now pursued their work in enforced absence and with uncertainty of return.

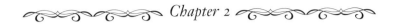

Mental Pictures and Visual Art: Aby Warburg and Emanuel Loewy

I

To find an approach shared by psychoanalysis and art history one has perhaps to look no further than the shelves within Aby Warburg's library. At the turn of the century Warburg, who had relinquished his claim to succeed his father as head of one of the most successful banking firms in Germany, had for several years been living in Florence as a private scholar. In 1900 he convinced his brothers to finance the creation of a private research library for the cultural sciences—a collection to be housed in his Hamburg residence and to consist of his own acquisitions. Four years later Warburg reluctantly left Florence and reestablished himself permanently in Hamburg, where he opened his library to a small circle of researchers and art historians. The hermitic scholar thus embarked on a path familiar to Lessing, the librarian at Wolfenbüttel. In 1913 Fritz Saxl arrived in Hamburg to work as Warburg's assistant; during the years immediately following the First World War—the period of Warburg's mental crisis and his recovery at the Kreuzlingen clinic in Switzerland—Saxl served as the library's acting director. In 1920, in keeping with Warburg's vision and with the brothers' support, Saxl began to transform the diverse, private collection into a research institute open to a wider academic public, sponsoring lectures and seminars, awarding stipends to researchers, and issuing its own *Studies* in art history. The recently founded University of Hamburg conferred upon Warburg an honorary professorship in 1921, thus enabling him after his return from Kreuzlingen in 1924 to lead student seminars at the library. By the time of his return home, the Warburg Library's collection and symposia had begun to draw professors from the new university, most notably the art historian Erwin Panofsky and the philosopher Ernst Cassirer. In 1926, the institution moved into its own building, adjacent to Warburg's home and adopted the official name Warburg Library of Cultural Science, inscribing above the entry to its precincts: *Mnemosyne*. Throughout those transformations the heart of Warburg's endeavor remained the book collection, whose system of classification originated in his own method of organizing his private shelves. As Saxl recalled, his mentor

> spoke of the 'law of the good neighbour.' The book of which one knew was in most cases not the book which one needed. The unknown neighbour on the shelf contained the vital information, although from its title one might not have guessed this. The overriding idea was that the books together—each containing its larger or smaller bit of information and being supplemented by its neighbours—should by their titles guide the student to perceive the essential forces of the human mind and its history.[1]

At the time that Warburg began the creation of his research library, Sigmund Freud in Vienna published *The Interpretation of Dreams* in which he wrote that

> dreams take into account in a general way the connection which undeniably exists between all the portions of the dream-thoughts by combining the whole material into a single situation or event. They reproduce *logical connection* by *simultaneity in time*. Here they are acting like the painter who, in a picture of the School of Athens or of Parnassus, represents in one group all the philosophers or all the poets. It is true that they were never in fact assembled in a single hall or on a single mountain-top; but they certainly form a group in the conceptual sense.[2]

Freud concluded: "Dreams carry this method of reproduction down to details. Whenever they show us two elements close together, this guarantees that there is some specially intimate connection between what correspond to them among the dream-thoughts."[3] Raphael's famous *School of Athens* joined the philosophers of ancient times in a vast public meeting

3. Raphael, *The School of Athens.* Stanza della Segnatura, Vatican Palace. Photo: Scala/Art Resource, New York.

hall; his *Parnassus* gathered poets of antiquity with those of the Italian Renaissance on the mountain of Apollo, in the presence of the god and his Muses (Figures 3 and 4). Both creations belonged to those frescoes which Raphael painted for the Vatican's *Stanza della Segnatura*, the room in which the Papal Court of Justice met, but also where Pope Julius II, who commissioned the artworks, may well have kept a private library.[4]

A union across time of the philosophers and poets of Greece and Italy: a fitting image for a Renaissance library. What is more, that image allows one to recognize in Aby Warburg's modern research library the creation of his own work of art. Warburg's library not only established a collection which offered researchers a new reserve of material to meet their

4. Raphael, *Parnassus*. Stanza della Segnatura, Vatican Palace. Photo: Scala/Art Resource, New York.

distinct interests, but perhaps even more important, it represented a careful composition which invited observers to visualize the interrelationships between each of its elements. Like Raphael, Warburg expected that the visitor to his collection would perceive the works of scholars, poets, and artists, however widely separated in time, according to the law of the good neighbor. But like Freud in Vienna, he also asked that the user seek within the library's interconnected materials their psychological construction and unity. Indeed, at each stage of his own research, Warburg expanded and rearranged his private shelves so as to mark newly discovered pathways and connections.[5]

The mental paths which led from volume to volume reached into humanity's primordial past. Having early in his career examined the significance of motion in painting, Warburg ultimately explored pagan magical practices, finally preparing a history of images—the *Mnemosyne*—which proposed to trace visual memory to its primal origins. In the closing paragraphs of his biography of Warburg, E. H. Gombrich chose to compare the art historian to the founder of psychoanalysis, pointing out that

> Thomas Mann once characterized Freud's position as exceptional, for Freud knew of the dark side of the psyche but sided with reason. The same is certainly true of Warburg. Like Freud, he was not an optimist. He was not sure that reason would ever win a permanent victory over unreason. But he conceived it as his task—sometimes perhaps naively overrating his own resources—to assist the struggle for enlightenment precisely because he knew the strength of the opposing camp.[6]

Warburg organized the tools and energies of his own camp within his Hamburg library. His scholarly collection produced a vision with which to confront and control psychological survivals of magic and the irrational, a function which once belonged to the classical amphitheater.

II

During his first years as an art historian Aby Warburg concerned himself most closely with the problem of how painters represented movement. His dissertation, published in 1893, examined specifically how Botticelli conveyed the sensation of motion in his two masterpieces, *The Birth of Venus* and *Primavera* (Figures 5 and 6). His intense interest in the problem of how images expressed a sense of movement provided a recurring stimulus to Warburg's psychological explorations of art, his investigations of ritual, and his search for a theory of memory.

5. Sandro Botticelli, *The Birth of Venus*. Florence, Galleria degli Uffizi. Photo: Alinari/Art Resource, New York.

To interpret images of movement in Botticelli's two paintings Warburg sought to explain the role of the classical nymphs, or Graces— the young, female figures whose postures, gestures, and drapery danced gently before the eyes of the spectator. As Warburg interpreted Botticelli's creative process, the painter first developed a mental picture of his mythological subjects from poetic descriptions, supplied chiefly by the Florentine humanist, Poliziano. In scenes which Poliziano recreated from Ovid's poems the painter found descriptions of the dancelike attributes of the Horae—the goddesses of the seasons who served as companions to Venus and as agents of nature. When envisioning the Graces the painter incorporated the humanist poet's depiction of "accessory forms in motion"[7]—drapery and hair fluttering with a breath of wind or with the steps of a dance. As Gombrich described, Warburg "sought to find out how

6. Sandro Botticelli, *Primavera*. Florence, Galleria degli Uffizi. Photo: Alinari/Art Resource, New York.

Botticelli and his patrons imagined antiquity, what ideas were evoked in their minds by the stories they read in Ovid and in Ovid's Renaissance imitators."[8] Thus did Warburg endeavor to document the mental images which provided common sources of both poetry and painting—and perhaps also, as Edgar Wind suggested, himself open a new path for their return.

While Botticelli did not intend to manufacture whole cloth his own visions of mythic scenes, neither did he expect to translate directly onto canvas the poetic imagery of Poliziano, who served as humanist adviser on the two paintings. Rather, the artist aimed at a "freer version,"[9] a creative effort shared in the beginning by painter, adviser, and patron, but a labor for which Botticelli resorted independently to ancient sources. To recreate a mythological scene Botticelli required not only poetic but also visual models of the movement which he sought to represent—models which he discovered in sculptural fragments from antiquity. Figures in motion such as appeared in the two paintings of Venus and her entourages survived in ancient relief sculptures and on Roman sarcophagi. In early Renaissance painting Botticelli thus demonstrated "the tendency, shaped by what was then known of antiquity, to turn to the arts of the ancient world whenever life was to be embodied in outward motion."[10]

Yet, the visual examples which most strongly impressed the painter of Venus and her companions belonged to the dramatic arts of his own day. Warburg considered it probable that in theatrical performances, perhaps in *Orfeo*, Poliziano's dramatic rendition of the myth of Orpheus, Botticelli had observed scenes, costumes, and figures—specifically, nymphs— similar to those the artist included in *The Birth of Venus* and *Primavera*. As Warburg stressed, such "festive performances set the characters before the artist's eyes as living, moving beings."[11] Noting Warburg's emphasis on the painter's attendance at dramatic enactments, Gombrich observed: "Perhaps the importance Warburg attached to ancient statuary which the artist may have actually seen springs from a similar conviction that the essence of painting is always mimetic."[12] For Warburg mimesis in connection with Botticelli's paintings thus derived from the festive and theatrical restorations of absent figures. The painter sought representations of mythological characters and events in specific material forms or dramatic reenactments. Further, through his own images the artist intended both to re-create the sensation of a single motion and, as in a theater performance, to transmit a quality of living movement to his scenes as a whole. Relying upon theatrical models and festive inspiration mimesis in painting not only reproduced a moment of action but embodied an emotional force from the stage.

The mimetic aspect of Botticelli's paintings consisted also in their relationship to an actual historical figure or event. According to Warburg, Botticelli's female figures of spring memorialized and transfigured the death of the young Simonetta dei Vespucci, whose likeness they bore. In *Primavera* Venus adopted a posture of sadness in the presence of the graceful figure of Spring, and thus did the goddess "amid the eternally youthful denizens of her realm, point to the transient earthly reflection of her power."[13] Yet by elevating Simonetta, the object of Giuliano de' Medici's adoration, into the embodiment of spring, the painter at the same time transformed the lost love object into "the consolatory personification of renewal."[14] Thus did Botticelli's paintings include not only a portion of dramatic enactment but also the memory of a deeply mourned loss. Having linked originally imaginary scenes to both a stage performance and an actual experience of grieving, Botticelli ultimately translated those scenes into images of movement and pictorial memories: reenactment and remembrance survived in the visual accessories of motion. The mental pictures with which the artist had begun the creation of his paintings proved to be the first steps toward the rediscovery of an ancient drama and the restoration of an absent object.

As Botticelli's example revealed, the influence of the ancient world reached early Renaissance artists when, in Warburg's words, antiquity "directs their attention to the most difficult problem in all art, which is that of capturing images of life in motion."[15] Yet, the attempt to represent movement in painting expressed not only a classical force but also a primal one. According to Warburg, Leon Battista Alberti warned in his *Libro della Pittura* of the primordial impulse that resurfaced with the depiction of movement:

> On the one hand, he is glad to see hair and garments in marked movement, and he gives rein to his fancy, attributing organic life to inanimate accessory forms; at such moments he sees snakes tangling, flames licking, or the branches of a tree. On the other hand, however, Alberti expressly insists that in depicting such motifs the painter keep his analogical wits about him sufficiently to avoid being tempted into unnatural excess, and that he set his accessory forms in motion only where the wind really might have caused such motion.[16]

Through images of movement the way led to the primal sources of classical art and culture. In the case of Botticelli's Graces or nymphs, such images included a softly raised hand, a gentle glance, a graceful turn, and a delicate, voluptuous step. As Warburg explained in his 1905 essay, "Dürer and Italian Antiquity," Renaissance artists come to regard such gestures as formulas through which to infuse their own works with not only movement but emotional energy. Expressive gestures depicted the primal emotive content of a moment of action. From the analysis of motion Warburg thus shifted to a study of the cultural migration of such formulaic images.

Criticizing Johann Winckelmann's famous association of Greek classical culture with the attributes of noble simplicity and quiet grandeur, Warburg argued in his essay on Dürer that "Italian artists had seized on the rediscovered antique treasury of forms just as much for its emotive force of gesture as for any tranquil, classic ideal."[17] In Dürer's engraving of the death of Orpheus the artist fell under the influence of "the emotive gestural language defined by Greece for this same tragic scene,"[18] language which Dürer learned from Italian art on his sojourns to the south (Figure 7). Such language or gesturing from antiquity not only imparted a sense of natural motion to a fragment of action but also expressed the impulsive or passionate content of that fragment. To describe those gestures which embodied an action or passion Warburg applied the term *Pathosformel*—pathos formula.[19] In the portrayal of Orpheus, whose brutal death completed "the dark mystery play of Dionysian legend,"[20] such gestures—his arm raised and knee bent in helpless defense—transmitted formulas for the depiction of tragic suffering. The ancient formula of the dying Orpheus which survived in Greek vase painting reappeared in a Venetian woodcut illustration of the Orphic legend as recounted by Ovid. Poliziano's dramatization of the same legend reinforced the cultural and psychological impact of the ancient Orphic gestures on a Renaissance audience who observed the fate of Orpheus "acted out"[21] upon the humanist poet's stage. Ancient emotive gestures mesmerized Dürer, who integrated them within his engraving of Orpheus but who in his later work subordinated them to the control of his own search for "composure."[22] The ancient formulas of gesture thus gave birth to a "migrant rhetoric," a language which provided means for "the interchange of artistic culture, in the fifteenth century, between past and present, and between North and South."[23] The image of Orpheus revealed the roots of the language of gesture in a primordial tragic mystery.

Examining the burial chapel of Francesco Sassetti—Lorenzo de' Medici's close friend and business associate—Warburg discovered a Renaissance theater for presenting that primal mystery. In the church of Santa Trinita the chapel's artistic formulas revived remnants of pagan

7. Albrecht Dürer, *Death of Orpheus*. Hamburg, Kunsthalle. Photo: Foto Marburg/Art Resource, New York.

dramaturgy and gesture. As with Botticelli's paintings, the mental image with which to decipher those formulas survived within a written document, in this case, Sassetti's last testament. In the final letter to his sons the patriarch conjured the mental picture of a tempestuous Fortune and urged his heirs to protect their inheritance against her effects: as Warburg wrote of Sassetti's imagery, "Fortune stood before his mind's eye as a personification of a hostile world, a capricious wind demon."[24] That same image surfaced in the heraldry of the merchant, Giovanni Rucellai, who had Fortune engraved on his crest as a female figure holding fast to a wind-filled sail. Rucellai's engraver applied "his Albertian sense of the grace of fluttering accessory forms"[25] to the design of the emblem, but those antique forms now also recalled a primal image—a vision of "Storm-Fortune, whose uncanny ability to switch from daemon of destruction to bountiful goddess fostered the atavistic image of her single, anthropomorphic, mythical identity."[26] Thus did ancient formulas of movement simultaneously represent boundless forces of regeneration and pitiless agents of ruin.

Rucellai perceived Fortune as "a symbol of energy"[27]—including the inward energy which he channeled into earthly action and success. Sassetti chose the centaur as the symbol of his own active life. Figures of centaurs appeared in the relief sculpture of Sassetti's tomb, where their energy was "unleashed, in all its antique gestural vehemence,"[28] gestures for which models existed on surviving Roman sarcophagi and in sketches of the Parthenon metopes. On the Sassetti sarcophagus a centaur accompanied the depiction of military games, and appeared with a group of Dionysian mourners who enacted "their forbidden excesses of orgiastic grief."[29] Within the chapel's carvings and frescoes, however, images of "pious Christian lamentation"[30] and heralds of the triumph of Christianity in the ancient world overarched the tomb itself, most sublimely in Ghirlandaio's fresco of the nativity. Joining pagan dynamism and medieval Christian devotion, the design of the Sassetti funeral chapel created a "symbolism of energy, synthesis, and balance."[31] That design projected into the surroundings of the tomb itself "the organic polarity that existed within the capacious mind of one cultivated early Renaissance man: a man who, in an age of transformed self-awareness, strove for a positive balance of his own."[32] Francesco Sassetti endured his inner conflict by attaining to self-knowledge, but ultimately found means for externalizing that conflict in the construction and figures of his chapel, transforming a Renaissance church into a setting for his own dramatic presentations. Indeed, as portrayed high on the wall of the chapel in Ghirlandaio's fresco of the confirmation of the Franciscan order, Sassetti and Lorenzo de' Medici, who himself exhibited "the air of a writer-director,"[33] wait on stage for Lorenzo's sons and teachers to join them (Figure 8). Lorenzo's entourage climbs onto the contested world platform that is made visible within the church as a part of "Sassetti's stock company."[34]

Renaissance art expressed contemporary cultural tensions and private struggles by reviving the spirit and techniques of ancient dramaturgy. When painters depicted from pagan art the dancelike, sensuous movements of young women, they summoned the joyfulness of natural grace and the expressive movements of pagan dramaturgy; and just as on the ancient stage, the postures of celebratory dance also recalled the maddened, grief-stricken intoxication of maenads, the female followers of Dionysos. Warburg's pathos formulas embodied both self-contained movement and, in Gombrich's words, "the primeval urge for unrestrained motion."[35] In the Sassetti chapel the centaur—who, as Gombrich stated, "speaks the language of pagan violence"[36]—reminded the visitor to the tomb that complete instinctual abandonment served as the agent of a destructive destiny. According to Warburg, Sassetti optimistically persuaded himself that in the projections of his own chapel "he had laid the unquiet spirits of antiquity to rest."[37] Those who visited the chapel of the Renaissance figure, however, perhaps felt themselves to have reentered the world of the amphitheater, in which classical actors had once simulated the presence of restless ancient spirits, cautioning the audience to observe their imitative creations from a distance.

In the paintings of Botticelli and Dürer, the plays of Poliziano, and the carvings of the Sassetti chapel, the pathos formula—or to use Lessing's words, the "visible arrested action"[38]—served as a vehicle of both regression and renewal. Bernd Roeck described its dynamic and ambivalent quality: "The memory trace which comes from antiquity is charged with energy that drives the process of the emancipation of humanity; it harbors at the same time, however, demonic menaces, residues of 'Dionysian'

8. Domenico Ghirlandaio, *Confirmation of the Franciscan Rule by Pope Honorius III.* Florence, Santa Trinita. Photo: Scala/Art Resource, New York.

antiquity."[39] Typical gestures or fragments of motion preserved the ancient dramatic movements which transformed delirium into a stage action. In their own images of movement pagan artists had successfully repeated that transformation, and recorded its emblems. Thus the Renaissance painter who employed pagan gestures revived that ancient confrontation with destructive passions, risking his own sense of self to reacquire the mastery achieved within the amphitheater. The pathos formula not only worked the remnant of an action into a visual type but regenerated the mental tension associated with a forbidding and sublime dramaturgic task, and sustained thereby the psychological afterlife of antiquity.

The gesture or movement which revived an ancient dramatic activity also recalled a world of pagan magical belief. The ties which connected painting to magic revealed themselves in the Renaissance fascination with astrological imagery and symbolism, a fascination which Warburg explored in the frescoes of the Palazzo Schifanoia in Ferrara, presenting his findings to the 1912 International Congress of Art Historians in Rome. The figures in the Schifanoia frescoes claimed ancient ancestors, but determining their lineage required that Warburg undo the distortions of their images and locate their place in the zodiacal system. The man gripping a rope, whose figure belonged to the month of March, derived from a classical Greek image of Perseus, which Egyptian and Indian cultures adopted as one of the zodiacal figures known as decans (Figure 9). The reworked figure of the Indian decan entered Persian, Arabic, and French sources before ultimately resurfacing, much transformed from its Greek origins, in Italian humanist manuscripts and the Ferrara mural. Above the level of the decans, the Schifanoia murals represented the planets with resurrected visions of the Olympian gods, now removed from terrestrial ties and glorified on a new platform as astrological deities. In the April fresco Venus reappeared in the heavens in the company of the Graces: for Warburg, "above all the three Graces, who are certainly copied from an antique original, prove the artist's intention of supplying an authentic reconstruction of antiquity."[40] In the Palazzo Schifanoia the process of return thus unfolded on two separate stages located above the arena of the human theater of action.

By pressing the classical images of the gods into the service of astrology the zodiacal system of the Palazzo Schifanoia produced "a transitional type between international Middle Ages and Italian Renaissance."[41] Further, where artists joined the gods and mythic ancestors of Greece to astrological signs and figures, that conflict which expressed itself in ancient pathos formulas gained new intensity. In Botticelli's paintings of Venus, the graceful movements, inward composure, and comprehending gaze of the Greek deities represented a sense of freedom and "the reawakening of nature."[42] In astrological thinking that tranquil and liberating sense

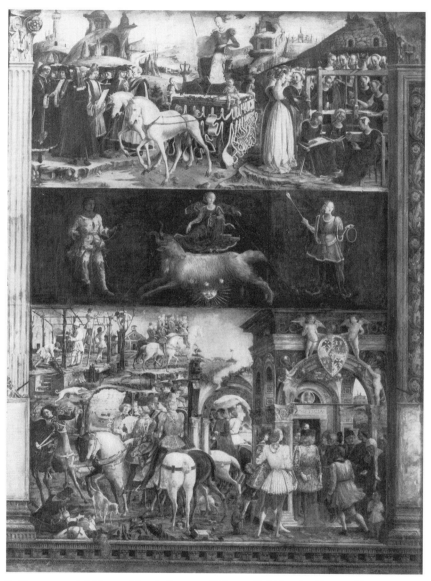

9. Francesco del Cossa, *March*. Ferrara, Palazzo Schifanoia. Photo: Alinari/Art Resource, New York.

became merged with a fear of uncontrollable, instinctive forces, destructive of both external equilibrium and inward peace. In the Sassetti chapel and the Palazzo Schifanoia, magical emblems and visual art combined to create enduring pictures of the split both within the energy of nature and within the human ego.

Analysis of the Schifanoia frescoes demonstrated for Warburg the centrality of art history to a "historical psychology of human expression."[43] Two years before the outbreak of the First World War he informed the participants in the Rome conference that by tracing the survival and transmission of images, art history "can range freely, with no fear of border guards, and can treat the ancient, medieval, and modern worlds as a coherent historical unity."[44] Renaissance art itself formed "part of an international process of dialectical engagement with the surviving imagery of Eastern Mediterranean pagan culture."[45] By restoring ancient images Renaissance painters reanimated a psychological drama with primal and universal roots. Art historians could follow the manifestations of that tragedy through the language of "internationally migrating images."[46] The events of 1914 quickly shattered the program of an internationalist corps of art scholars tracking images across borders of time and place.

III

In the years of postwar European recovery and of his private convalescence Warburg reentered the intellectual world of the Palazzo Schifanoia. In the Ferrarese palace Renaissance painting had revealed its susceptibility to primal, magical visions but also its ability to control such visions as elements of a dramatic tension. At Kreuzlingen, far from the prewar surroundings of Ferrara, Warburg reexplored magical thinking and dramatic consciousness as expressed not in a Renaissance palazzo but on a Pueblo ceremonial stage, offering his conclusions in a 1923 lecture composed from materials which he gathered on his research journey to New Mexico and Arizona in 1895 and 1896.[47] During that earliest inquiry into religious and clan traditions, Warburg encountered in the *Hemis Kachina* dance not merely an example of pagan ritual performance but an instance of ancient dramaturgy. The dance, which masked performers executed in an open-air plaza and which spectators viewed from positions above the performance area, re-created the presence of absent figures—the *kachinas*, or ancestral spirits (Figures 10 and 11). The Pueblo rite, which both encouraged a successful crop and completed the initiation of youths into ceremonial societies, united magical practices and clan customs with enactments reminiscent of the "tragic chorus."[48] The *Hemis Kachina* ceremony thus appeared to Warburg as a singular union of primitive and classical survivals—"the dramatic magical dance, actually returned to life."[49] Having witnessed that dance, Warburg could not resist accompanying the performers to their off-stage precinct—or *scene* in the language of the Greek amphitheater—and himself donning a mask[50] (Figure 12). Upon his return to Hamburg, the traveler conceived of issuing his own photographic and written commentary on the dance—a performance which appealed not only to his newly acquired anthropological interest, but also to his classical dramaturgic sensibility. In the event, he finally fulfilled his ambition through the lecture delivered at Binswanger's Swiss refuge.[51]

For his audience of Kreuzlingen physicians and patients Warburg described how the ritual enactments and religious images of the Pueblos evoked both a magical, intoxicating reaction and a consoling, "sober purposiveness."[52] To accomplish "the binding of hostile natural forces"[53] the Pueblos sought to forge an identity between themselves and the unforgiving powers of nature. In ritual dances participants donned the masks of those objects over which they sought mastery: "When the hunter or tiller of the soil masks himself, transforms himself into an imitation of his booty—be that animal or corn—he believes that through mysterious, mimic transformation he will be able to procure in advance what he coterminously strives to achieve through his sober, vigilant work as tiller and hunter."[54] In assuming the identity of an animal, however, the dancer not only adopted that being's visage, but imitated its movements, and thus performed a complete self-transformation. According to Warburg, the "pantomimic animal dance" represented not only "a cultic act of the highest devotion" but the "self-abandon to an alien being."[55] To imitate through masked enactment meant to risk sacrificing completely one's own identity, a risk inherent to all magic. Ritual mimesis thus contained both a

10. Aby Warburg, Hemis Kachina dance at Oraibi, Arizona, May 1896. London, Warburg Institute, Photographic Collection. Photo: University of London, Warburg Institute.

sublime achievement and a grave danger: attaining identification in movement threatened the actor with the loss of self.[56]

How did the Pueblos—and humanity—overcome the danger within magical practices? Symbolic identifications gradually replaced identity in movement and gesture: in religion it became "a question of establishing a

11. Aby Warburg, Hemis Kachina dance at Oraibi, Arizona, May 1896. London, Warburg Institute, Photographic Collection. Photo: University of London, Warburg Institute.

bond between natural forces and man, of creating a symbol as the connecting agent, indeed as the magical rite that achieves integration by sending out a mediator."[57] For the Pueblos, the most effective and most sacred mediator remained the serpent, the image of which pervaded Pueblo life and religion. The evolution of the serpent image revealed itself in remnants of a more ancient ritual practice which still survived among Pueblos: the

12. Aby Warburg donning a Hemis Kachina mask at Oraibi, Arizona, May 1896 (photographer unknown). London, Warburg Institute, Photographic Collection. Photo: University of London, Warburg Institute.

dance with living snakes. That ceremonial performance, which demonstrated the "magical desire for unity with nature via the animal world,"[58] recalled "not the imitation of the animal but the bluntest engagement with it as a ritual participant."[59] During the earliest phase of religious practice the serpent embodied the demonic, violent powers of nature and served as the object of sacrificial rites. Over time, however, the snake became perceived as a hallowed object of imitation and devotion—a being capable of passing from the earth and the realm of the dead into the skies so as to produce life-giving rains. From a sacred creature which ascended to the heavens it developed finally into a symbolic image of ethereal aspirations. Through the use of such symbols the individual both preserved the boundaries between the self and nature and communicated the highest aspirations of the personality.

In the evolution of ritual and symbolism among the Pueblos Warburg perceived the outlines of a universal, historical pattern: the sublimation of paganism. The transformation of the serpent ritual in Pueblo culture thus illuminated the history of the cult of Asclepius, the god of healing in the Western world. Pagan antiquity worshipped Asclepius first in the guise of a serpent—that being which emerged from the world of the dead with new life—and only later adopted him as that god who kept with him a healing scepter around which a snake wrapped itself as the symbol of renewal. Medieval Europe elevated the god into the heavens as an astrological deity. The serpent as a symbol of healing and new life reappeared in later Christian imagination—proof of the "indestructibility of the memory of the serpent cult"[60]—but instead as a spiritual reminder of humanity's early misapprehension of the true meaning of redemption.

Pueblo ceremonial and the cult of Asclepius demonstrated that religion evolved through the metamorphosis of pagan rites in which participants originally identified themselves with powers of nature. In dance the participant enacted that identity, "transforming himself personally into a prime causal agent in the order of things."[61] At the next stage of religious development mythology sublimated pagan identification: there occurred "the spiritualization of the bond between humans and alien beings."[62] Religion thus began to arrive at the conception of an autonomous spiritual self. Survival and expansion of that sense of autonomy required the pagan dramaturgic impulse, which utilized the mask not only to assist a physical, mimic simulation but also to create a symbolic contact with sacred objects. As Warburg concluded: "The will to devotional zeal is an ennobled form of the donning of a mask."[63] Both self-negation and spiritual self-assertion revealed origins in dramaturgic tendencies.

In Warburg's scheme of religious development, the world of antiquity occupied a pivotal yet ambiguous place. The Olympian gods marked a sublime creation, but that spiritual triumph did not dislodge primitive fears of the vengeful, violent power of nature. Both grandeur and terror expressed themselves in the primitive myth of Laocoon and the serpent, and in its later sculptural representation. The mythic story of the Trojan priest revived "the serpent as a destroying force from the underworld,"[64] sent by the gods to punish Laocoon for having warned Troy against accepting Greek promises, a punishment that fell not only on the priest but also on his sons. The famous Hellenistic sculpture of the defiant Laocoon and his young sons resisting the torment visited upon them by the gods embodied the figures' desperate autonomy: "Thus the death of the father and his sons becomes a symbol of ancient suffering: death at the hands of vengeful demons, without justice and without hope of redemption. That is the hopeless, tragic pessimism of antiquity."[65] Sculpture inherited the substance of ancient dramaturgy: the reencounter with suffering, not its overcoming.

From Warburg's outline of religious and cultural history emerges an art historical view of the links between pagan ceremony, tragic drama, and the art of painting. Ancient myths and tragedies spiritualized pagan rituals by replacing the powers of nature with the will of the gods. The mythic worldview, however, preserved the primeval fear of nature, and tragic drama remained closely tied to primitive rites through the imitation of an action in the form of action. Within the circle of the amphitheater classical performers recalled the primitive magical reliance on mimic behavior to control natural terrors and primordial fears. Yet, ideally, actors guarded a sphere of autonomy, protecting the distance between themselves and their objects of imitation, between their performance area and the audience. The visual arts sustained the primal attempt at achieving identity with nature, but much reduced the danger to the personality: painting and sculpture originated as objects of inward contemplation—mental pictures—and even after being transferred to canvas or stone those pictures remained objects of removed reflection to both artist and spectator. The fragment of motion or expressive gesture in painting—the pathos formula—reproduced a portion of pagan dance, but also a trace

of the amphitheater. Indeed, painting most securely upheld the boundaries of identity, and in that achievement resided its redemptive quality.
In Warburg's words, "the seeker of redemption" advanced from "instinctual, magical interaction to a spiritualized taking of distance."[66] That distance which the playwright and actor generated on the dramatic stage the
painter adopted and expanded in his work on canvas, a type of distance
which Warburg characterized in his lecture notes as *Denkraum*, or reflective space.[67]

In his analysis of the unpublished notes to the Kreuzlingen lecture,
Gombrich explored Warburg's concern with the psychology of the ego
and the boundaries of identity. The lecture notes concentrated on ties
between image-making and the psychological mechanism of projection.
To reduce the intensity of its phobic fears, primitive humanity projected
onto the threatening, incomprehensible powers of nature the images of
known beings. Image-making marked the first stage in which civilization
imposed an order upon the external world, the foundation upon which
humanity developed a comprehension of the world through symbols; from
symbolic understanding, human beings finally arrived at the formulation
of rational laws. Still, as Gombrich emphasized: "In Warburg's view the
'phobic reflex of cause projection' is always lingering on the threshold
of our consciousness."[68] Memory preserved not only those images which
allowed the ego to recognize a rational order in the external world but
also the images which the primitive ego had originally projected outward
in constructing a world of its own invention. Thus did memory harbor
a dual tendency: one tendency preserved the boundary between the ego
and the world, and protected reflective reasoning; the other abolished that
boundary, and revived the primordial attempt at identifying with a world
alien and threatening to the ego.

In the private notes and drafts which he prepared for lectures or
future manuscripts, Warburg in his final years examined further the conflicting tendencies of memory. Those opposing forces appeared vividly
within the pathos formula. The gesture of pathos recalled the pagan sacrifice of the self to rituals of movement. Such a formula, however, did
not inevitably represent a loss of self but instead could embody a moment

of self-recognition, or the consciousness of how one's actions fit within a wider drama.[69] Images or symbols in painting preserved the demonic energies of paganism, and the artists who worked with such images inevitably revived primeval, instinctive passions in their works—and in themselves. Pagan impulses in art thus gave renewed life to antiquity, but just as they had threatened the personality of the mimic dancer, they also endangered the personality of the artist. The successful painter redirected those energies—sublimated them—toward the spiritual and moral contemplation of symbols.

Warburg appropriately entitled his last, unpublished project, *Mnemosyne*—Memory. In that never-completed work Warburg planned, in his own words, to create a picture atlas. That atlas, with accompanying commentary, would assemble the chief artistic and symbolic images comprising the collective memory of Western civilization. Warburg began to organize the atlas around shared themes or formulas. On a single screen he joined images visually related but separated by centuries of history and in that way emphasized the common memory and energy which linked them across time. With this project Warburg ceased to emphasize the process of historical change but concentrated on the mechanics of remembrance and the psychological survival of images. According to the perspective of *Mnemosyne*, the dual nature of memory determined the pattern of history: "rhythmical change between the identification with the object and the return to detachment."[70] Thus, each period of history confronted anew the choice between conflicting psychological responses to the world: pagan abandonment or moral, redemptive aspiration. Renaissance artists demonstrated how human beings safely drew upon primal energies by channeling them toward spiritual attainments. The "fate of human civilization"[71] depended upon the ability of later generations to learn from that model.

According to Gombrich, *Mnemosyne* revealed "the memories of a scholar's life as if they were woven into a dream."[72] The organization of the project certainly bore comparison to the dream work: ideas and reactions separated by historical time became united within single images. *Mnemosyne* also called to mind that system of classification which Warburg had already employed within his library: the law of the good neighbor.

Thus did Warburg organize his final work according to that method of remembrance common to paintings, dreams, and libraries—a method also employed by Raphael.

IV

Aby Warburg's approach to art history and psychology combined ritualist and classicist elements in an evolving pattern. Early in his career Warburg concerned himself with the problem of how Renaissance paintings created the illusion of living movement. To explain the sense of motion in painting he traced the origins of artworks to mental pictures, in which the artist revisualized gestures of movement, or pathos formulas. When the painter translated a mental vision onto canvas, the pathos formula gave to his work an essentially mimetic quality: it embodied the fragment of a drama, a fragment which conveyed emotional force. The Renaissance artist reproduced that portion of dramatic action as it had reappeared in classical sculpture, or as it reemerged in contemporary theatrical performance. The pathos formula, however, also communicated an image of movement traceable to primitive mimic rituals, and to their tendencies toward primal identification with nature and self-abandonment. Image-making thus became a mechanism of remembrance which threatened the loss of self. Yet, the creation of images also marked an essential act of sublimation, or spiritualization, and therefore promised the final recovery, or redemption, of the self. As *Mnemosyne* claimed, the primitive passions and sublimated aspirations of humanity remained in conflict within all surviving images: thus did memory make of the pathos formula an image of recurrent human suffering.

In Vienna, Emanuel Loewy sought to interpret image-making as a function of memory, and through art to chart the shifts in types of memory from primitive to classical civilization. When E. H. Gombrich published *Art and Illusion* in 1960 he dedicated the book to Ernst Kris; to his advisor in art history at the University of Vienna, Julius von Schlosser; and to his professor in ancient studies, Emanuel Loewy. In his own book, Gombrich drew attention to his teacher's masterwork, *The Rendering of*

Nature in Early Greek Art, through which "Loewy taught us to appreciate the forces which have to be overcome by an art aiming at the illusion of reality."[73] Loewy also became teacher to Sigmund Freud. As Ernest Jones recorded, Freud met regularly with the classicist on Loewy's return trips from Rome.[74] Loewy remained Freud's oldest friend. Both grew up and attended school in Vienna's Leopoldstadt district, home to the majority of struggling Austro-Hungarian Jews who, like the fathers of both Freud and Loewy, emigrated to the capital from within Habsburg territories. The students did not meet, however, until Freud's first year at the university, probably in Theodor Gomperz's lectures on ancient philosophy, which Loewy, in his last year of gymnasium, attended, as did Freud.[75] In 1887, Loewy became a lecturer in classical archeology at the University of Vienna, and two years later received an international chair in archeology and the history of ancient art at the University of Rome. The First World War forced Loewy in 1915 to return permanently to the Austrian capital, where he continued his teaching but did not resume writing until several years after the peace. In February 1938, Loewy died in Vienna, one month before the *Anschluss* with Nazi Germany.[76]

In *The Rendering of Nature in Early Greek Art,* published in 1900, Loewy analyzed artifacts of Greek sculpture, reliefs, and vase painting from the Archaic Age, prior to the advent of naturalism in fifth-century Greek art. The ancient scholar concerned himself specifically with the question of how, in the years before the revolutionary triumphs of Greek realism, painters and sculptors attempted to imitate works of nature in their art. By answering that question Loewy intended also to illuminate the psychology of image-making and, further, to demonstrate the survival of the archaic mentality within the highest accomplishments of Greek classicism. As with the case of Warburg, Loewy's interest in the psychological meaning of art led him to an interpretation of primal mental processes and their persistence in image-making. In contrast to Warburg, the archaeologist and ancient scholar began not with an investigation of Italian Renaissance revivals of Greek classicism but with a direct exploration of the primitive underground from which classical culture arose in antiquity.

Like Warburg, Loewy believed that image-making in art had first to be understood not as a matter of technique or convention but as a psychological process of recollection. Images entered conscious memory first in the form of ideal types or models: "As the result of the visual impressions which we have received from numerous examples of the same object, there remains fixed in our minds a memory-picture, which is no other than the Platonic Idea of the object, namely, a typical picture, clear of everything individual or accidental."[77] From such primal, psychical formations—or "spontaneous memory-pictures"[78]—the archaic artist composed his creations. Those primitive memory-pictures, or prototypes, determined the form of archaic images, in the first place, their schematic, linear designs—what we perceive as stylized patterns. Further, having selected from an object its distinguishing feature, memory produced an image which "shows the form with the property that differentiates it from other forms."[79] Invariably such properties presented themselves to the mind from the widest possible angle—from that view which displayed them most fully. To keep such defining traits firmly within consciousness, the mind etched them with sharp contours. Finally, primitive recollection did not picture complex objects as organic, integrated wholes. Rather, spontaneous memory-pictures of the various parts of an object appeared as "a succession of images."[80] There remained in memory only those aspects of a figure necessary to "the clear consciousness of the object."[81]

Memory became drawn to movement—or "the animated and active features of a scene"[82]—but ignored the landscape or context of actions. Features of background or milieu appeared in recall as independent images, isolated from the activity to which they were joined in reality. Of motion itself memory constructed no lucid image. In trying to capture movement, "the mind's eye can grasp only the moments of relative rest."[83] Imagination attempted to organize those fragments "into such order as the moment of motion seized seemed to present."[84] Remembrance of objects and events in motion seemed to operate according to the procedure which Lessing had ascribed to poetry: the mind generated a succession of discrete images. From such a perspective, spontaneous memory followed more closely the laws of poetic imagination than the principles of observable reality.

How then did the sculptor or vase painter begin to develop a visual art? Archaic artists represented the external world not according to their immediate visual experiences but rather according to their primitive memory-pictures: "For along with the pictures that reality presents to the eye, there exists another world of images, living or coming into life in our minds alone, which, though indeed suggested by reality, are nevertheless essentially metamorphosed. Every primitive artist, when endeavoring to imitate nature, seeks with the spontaneity of a psychical function to reproduce merely these mental images."[85] Yet, that attempt to communicate memory-pictures by means of a tangible, visual art marked an essential step toward the achievement of genuine realism, and thus a radical turning point in cultural history. As Loewy concluded: "For the mere translation of the mental image into graphic form contains a revolutionary germ."[86] Expressed differently, an important shift had occurred from poetic imagination to artistic consciousness, paralleling the change from an epic to dramatic mode.

Archaic Greek drawing and sculpture embodied a fertile but still primitive stage in art. Artists designed vase paintings, reliefs, and even freestanding statues from spontaneous memory-pictures, modeling their works on the characteristics of such images. Objects appeared as types, depicted with sharply linear or stylized features. The painter or sculptor concentrated on producing the mere outlines or contours of objects, a tendency most strongly evident in silhouettes on vases and in the flatness of reliefs and statuary. All surfaces appeared as if exposed to a uniform light, without the application of shading or the gradation of tones. Artists dispensed with the correct proportions of figures, so as to present each part from the widest possible view, and distributed figures in their compositions without regard to visual perspective, permitting no object to interfere with the view of another. Finally, pre-classical figures conveyed no sense of living movement, their faces indicated little emotion, and their activities appeared divorced from their surroundings. Yet, archaic drawing and sculpture helped to prepare the way for the classical Greek revolution in naturalism.

How did an art which portrayed the depth, fullness, and individuality of objects, which employed natural perspective and correct proportion, which recognized the effects of light and shade, and which instilled even in figures of repose a sense of living motion—how did such an art of imitation emerge from primitive soil? During the Archaic Age, there began "accumulations of memory as unconscious preparation for the representation of what we see."[87] What Loewy referred to as "the common store"[88] of memory slowly expanded—and artists themselves began to add to that store. Loewy cited the example of changing depictions of the horse and chariot: to give the most complete view archaic artists invariably drew the animal and chariot from the side. In the case of two- and four-horse teams, artists chose the frontal view so as to provide an equal angle on each animal within the team. That view now became part of the stock of memory images to which later painters and sculptors could turn: "in the memory-pictures drawn from such works there may lie, perhaps, an explanation of the surprisingly early occurrence of chariots seen from the front, not only in high relief, but in low relief and drawing."[89] Thus primitive artists themselves not only contributed to the store of remembrance but also multiplied the angles of vision.

Still, classical art did not emerge simply as an evolutionary outgrowth of primitive vase painting, relief sculpture, and statuary. Indeed, two influences external to the work of painters and sculptors became decisive forces in the development of realism in the visual arts: the observation of nature and the evolution of drama. By the end of the archaic period, the growing interest in the direct examination of the natural world had already begun to transform art. New powers of observation not only expanded the store of recall but completed those images which had survived from primitive memory-pictures. The decisive turn came with the technique of foreshortening and the indication in art of the third dimension to figures: that advance represented "the first breaking away from the primary method of working entirely from the mental image. . . . With foreshortening the artist set to work for the first time upon a principle that conflicts with the primitive conception, and is derived from physical reality."[90] From the close study of nature there followed attempts to draw or sculpt rounded figures, to utilize shaded contours, and to introduce visual perspective. Thus classical artists finally freed themselves from merely assembling prototypical pictures and turned to the production of figures in their full individuality. In the visual arts, expansion of the powers of observation reflected "the awakening consciousness of plasticity."[91]

In Greek drawing and sculpture the awareness of plasticity expressed itself most clearly in the artist's new feeling for movement. Visual artists began to instill a sense of action in their creations, which they derived not only from immediate observation, but perhaps just as importantly from the works of Greek poets and dramatists. Lessing had emphasized that poets wove discrete pictures into an imagined continuity of living motion, whereas visual artists remained trapped by the forms of spontaneous memory. Guarding against any encroachment on the written word, the Enlightenment critic forbade painters from seeking their subject matter in poetry, especially in Homer, the source of poetic narrative. Yet, from Loewy's point of view, narrative poetry provided an initial, unique stimulus to realism in the visual arts: "In the effort to tell a story graphically there will be things to be represented for which the memory-pictures are entirely wanting. Such experiences would urge the draughtsman endowed with artistic energy to direct or indirect recourse to nature."[92] The accomplishment of conveying movement through visual art, however, demanded the construction of a scene, from which action drew a living quality. Such became the triumph of classical relief sculptures, which molded figures in depth and against the background of an identifiable milieu. The funereal relief, for example, moved toward the depiction of "a fuller family picture,"[93] and thus increased the number of represented figures from two persons to three, or even four. Increasingly animated scenes of absent kin required that additional family members be carved at new depths of distance within stone. As Arnold Hauser later wrote, toward the end of the archaic period funeral monuments had "shaken off all hieratic connections,"[94] relinquishing stylized, ceremonial appearances, and aiming instead at a thorough naturalism.

In Greece, classicism did not abolish archaic forms but revised and built upon them. The achievement of realism in the visual arts occurred in a succession of phases, with remnants of older phases surviving within later periods. In the case of the technique of foreshortening, for example, classical painters and sculptors began to depict parts of a figure from foreshortened angles but did not portray the entire object in natural perspective.

In statuary, after figures began to assume rounded contours, they continued to appear without physical depth. Even as painters and sculptors acquired new observations, techniques, and vantage points, "we see the artist welding them inorganically together, and not seldom grafting them on forms of the old type."[95] Prototypical models—the products of spontaneous memory—retained their grip upon the classical imagination: the Greek revolution in art occurred only after the accumulation of numerous modifications in archaic types. Throughout that long, cumulative process, primitive memory forms persisted or reappeared within classical artwork. By struggling with those reemergent forms, Greek painters and sculptors developed the artistic means through which to communicate a sense of living movement.

In that artistic struggle can one also detect the impact of the rise of tragic drama upon the visual arts, or at least the presence in relief sculpture of a process akin to that taking place in the theater? In the early classical period, Aeschylus added a second actor to his tragedies; Sophocles—and, it has been argued, perhaps Aeschylus before him—included a third personage. The greater complexity of scenes added new intensity and dimension to the conflicts and movements enacted on stage.[96] Perhaps that change in theatrical performance—that effort at creating a stage presence for absent objects—offered a model to the visual arts. As Loewy's analysis of family monuments demonstrated, not only the closer observation of nature but also the envisioning of dramatic scenes led archaic painters and sculptors toward a stricter imitation of reality.

V

When Loewy returned to scholarly writing after the First World War he explored not only the primitive forms but also the primal motivations within archaic artworks. Tracing the original motive forces of art led him into a world of primordial fears and dramaturgic energies, which he described in a lecture delivered before the Vienna Academy of Sciences. Presented in 1930, that lecture portrayed the archaic period as the crucible within which the effort at controlling primal fears through magic slowly metamorphosed into their mimetic enactment on stage before a circle of spectators.

As Loewy detailed, archaic art served as a protective, magical agent which confronted overwhelming natural forces and hostile unearthly powers with equally threatening and aggressive images. The successful operation of defensive, or apotropaic, images derived from their power of mimesis, or the power by which such images "simulate the presence of certain objects or beings whose appearance is supposed to act as a deterrent."[97] Drawings of bulls, lions, or snakes; of horse-drawn racing chariots; of medicinal plants and vegetation—all functioned as protective measures. So too did the ancient *Fratzengesichtern*[98]—grimacing or grotesque human visages and masks. By contrast, ancient religious supplicants accomplished defensive aims by presenting hostile agents with ritual offerings or gifts, especially gifts of that which possessed the image of beauty. Both grotesque and gentle expressions originated in primordial fears and self-protective intentions: the frequent combination of fearsome and friendly attributes within a single image only emphasized the open pathway which existed between grimaces and grace.

Images of movement and action depicted mythic struggles against hostile forces, but also preserved pictures of sacred combats and processions—ceremonies which aimed at protection and propitiation. Minoan frescoes portrayed the performance of the sacred bullfight, that primitive combat which functioned both as a magical rite and as a spectacle [*Schauspiel*][99] organized before an assembled audience. Representations of the performance aimed not only at reviving the practical magic of the ritual but at producing objects for display. To create an impressive visual exhibit the Minoan artist utilized naturalist techniques, incorporating elements of living surroundings and landscape into his frescoes. Minoan art thus provided a unique primitive example of how dramaturgic impulses led image-making from primitive, defensive purposes to the exercise of creativity for its own ends. The archaic period brought that artistic transformation to fulfillment, as finally exemplified in the triumphal construction of the Parthenon: "Just as in the Panathenaic procession the richest display of the most exalted defensive and propitiatory measures became the most glorious spectacle, so is its reproduction in the friezes surrounding the temple of the guardian goddess the supreme monumental summation of the intentions transmitted within the images and at the same time in the highest sense decorative and therefore free art."[100]

Whereas his early work interpreted stylized archaic forms as the survivals of primitive memory images, Loewy's lecture to the academy described stylization as an effort by image-makers to transform pictures into a new type of spectacle—an effort which at the conclusion of the archaic period accompanied the growth of dramatic performance. Thus the independent demands of the classical stage and spectator gave impetus not only to the movement toward naturalism but also to the renewed use of stylized renderings. Greek revolutionaries in visual art produced their work for audiences who, subject to primitive anxieties and magical expectations, began also to gather in ever greater numbers within the amphitheaters, and who, in Athens, could gaze directly above the Theater of Dionysos to view the Parthenon.

Having begun with the study of archaic Greek art, Loewy, like Warburg, imagined himself an observer of pagan dramatic spectacle. To be sure, fundamental differences existed between the two scholars. Warburg focused on the works of those Renaissance artists who, relying on examples from classical Greece, had mastered—or instead remastered—the representation of movement. Artistic formulas derived from images of motion. Such pictures recalled fragments of real enactments—fragments of pagan ritual which had survived in Greek classical culture. As a result, visual art preserved the psychological energy and conflicts which animated those rituals, and which presented simultaneously a danger and a redemptive promise to the self. Primitive mental impulses reemerged in the image of an action: such impulses infused that image with a feeling of movement.

In contrast to Warburg, Loewy examined not the rebirth of classical Greek artworks but the archaic art from which classicism had been born. He studied drawings, reliefs, and sculptures from the period before artists had fully conquered the imitation of nature and had achieved the realistic expression of movement. Like Warburg, he believed that artists built their works upon primal formulas, but those formulas Loewy interpreted as spontaneous memory-pictures or prototypical images. Archaic memory operated according to a process of "mental abstraction:"[101] the primitive mind conceived typical forms, discarding the expressive qualities and actions which belonged to real figures. Through a series of modifications, Greek artists slowly added indications of movement to the prototypes which they carried in memory. Primal images, as Loewy characterized them, call to mind not pagan dance but rather the stylized, hieratic element of sacred spectacle and tragic recitation.

Still, Loewy's work revealed a set of concerns which also became central to the early Warburgian school: the significance of scene construction in the Greek revolution in art; the meaning of a common stock of artistic images within the process of creation; and the importance of preexisting mental schema, and their gradual modification, in the evolution of image-making. Conceiving of art history and psychology as in part combined fields, Warburg and Loewy searched visual images for the remnants of archaic mental pictures. Within the visual arts they also perceived the residue of ancient dramatic enactments, a perception shared by Loewy's friend and colleague Sigmund Freud.

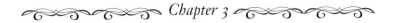

Reenactments: Sigmund Freud

I

The year 1900 marked a decisive point in the careers of both Aby Warburg and Emanuel Loewy. In 1900, Warburg set in process the creation of his library for cultural history—a scholarly precinct for exploring the afterlife of pagan antiquity. In the same year, Loewy published *The Rendering of Nature in Early Greek Art*, which put forward a new psychological theory of artistic consciousness. The work of both scholars helped to initiate an approach to cultural research which combined psychological science and art criticism. Both had begun their studies of art by seeking to explain the sense of living motion conveyed within visual images, a problem which ultimately led them to attempt the reconstruction of primal mentalities and actions. Despite differences in methodological approach—Warburg began with the fluid artwork of Renaissance Italy, Loewy with the angular creations of archaic Greece—they reached one similar conclusion: by incorporating traces of primitive designs and pagan spectacles into their art, classical Greek painters and sculptors—as well as their Renaissance imitators—preserved memories and mental attitudes from the remote past of humanity. Thus did Warburg and Loewy arrive at an answer to their original question: the sense of movement in mental pictures and visual representations developed from the artist's struggle with a reemerging past, whether that past surfaced in remnants of pagan performances and identities or in fragments of prototypical images.

In the same crucial year of 1900 Sigmund Freud published *The Interpretation of Dreams*, and thereby arrived at the turning point of his own career.[1] The book, which expounded not only Freud's method of dream interpretation but also a science of the mind, brought the study of images to the center of that science. Freudian interpretation delved into principles of visual and dramatic composition in dreams, discriminated among modes of representation, analyzed the construction of scenes, and explicated the techniques of image-making which yielded such unusual mental products. The psychoanalytic interpreter did not approach mental pictures as static, artificial constructions. In seeking the meaning of dreams, Freud, like Warburg, confronted instead the question of how images—in this case, dream images—came to embody a sense of living reality and natural movement.

Indeed, striking similarities existed between the trajectories which Freud and Warburg followed as cultural scientists. As with the art historian, Freud moved from the interpretation of pictorial images to the study of expressive motion and behavior. That transition began in 1905 with his book, *Jokes and their Relation to the Unconscious*, which applied to the language of jokes the psychoanalytic method of dream interpretation. The book's concluding sections focused on comedy, through which Freud explored "ideational mimetics,"[2] or the communication of ideas in movement and gesture. In 1907, when he applied dream analysis to a work of literature—Wilhelm Jensen's "Gradiva: A Pompeian Fantasy"—Freud's interests moved even nearer to those of Warburg. Both the plot of Jensen's story and its fictional hero's dream centered on an ancient bas relief of a young woman who, in the act of walking, had lightly gathered the folds of her dress in such manner that they gently followed her step. At the same instant she also raised the back of one of her feet so that only her toes touched the ground. In the image of Gradiva—as the story's protagonist named the sculpted figure—appeared a version of the classical nymph whom Warburg had analyzed in Botticelli's *Primavera*. Thus the interpretation of images in dreams, jokes, and literature had led Freud to the study of movement, and in the case of Jensen's Gradiva, to that gesture associated with the ancient Graces which Warburg had also made an object of scrutiny.

Indeed, in 1896 Freud had begun to build his private art collection by acquiring examples from Florence—"I have now," he wrote, "adorned my room with plaster casts of Florentine statues"[3]—and during the years immediately preceding the outbreak of the First World War he finally offered his own analyses of Renaissance painting and sculpture. Examining first the process of pictorial image-making—specifically through the smile and gestures of love which Leonardo da Vinci depicted in his paintings— he then explored traces of motion and their significance as fragments of action in Michelangelo's sculpture of the prophet Moses. Ultimately, his effort to understand the meaning of gesture and movement in Italian artwork led Freud to trace the reappearance of the ancient Graces on the Shakespearean stage.

As in Warburg's case, Freud's object of inquiry broadened from Renaissance image-making and theatrical performance to include primitive ritual behavior. In the essays comprising *Totem and Taboo*, published in 1912 and 1913, Freud analyzed primeval rituals as dramatic reenactments—the acting out not only of stories, emotions, and ideas but of historical events. The ceremony of the totem meal reproduced that event from which all religious and social institutions had developed: the killing of the father by the primal horde and the establishment of the community of brothers. Throughout the evolution of civilization fragments of the Oedipal crime reemerged in religious and social ceremonials. Such ritual revivals preserved collective memory of the primal deed and its consequences, and expressed thereby the identification of the brothers with each other as participants in the crime. At the same time such rites allowed the sons to reiterate their devotion to the father and convey their sense of identity not only with each other but with the original patriarch. As imitative creations, religious ceremonies and social rites thus provided means of remembrance and defined the complex, primal identities of both performers and audience. From those primordial rituals emerged the effort at dramatically restoring absent objects within the classical amphitheater.

From the turn of the century to the eve of the First World War, Freud's analysis of image-making thus expanded from dreams, comic movements, and literary inventions to images as enacted upon the theatrical stage, the religious altar, and the platform of history. His interest in how images conveyed a sense of living movement and immediate reality helped to direct psychoanalysis from individual to collective psychology. Not surprisingly, Freud finally accepted as the title of the first journal for the application of psychoanalysis to the cultural sciences the Latin designation *Imago*, a term which, in its ancient origins, referred to the products both of picture-making and of physical imitation. In *Imago*, which first appeared in 1912, Freud published his studies of Michelangelo's sculpture and of Shakespeare's drama, as well as the essays which formed *Totem and Taboo*. Beginning with the dream book, this chapter will trace the evolution of Freud's interpretation of image-making, from his analysis of mental pictures and expressive gestures to his exploration of ritual performances and the primal tragedy motivating such reenactments.

II

In his comparison of the dream work to Raphael's composition of the *School of Athens* and *Parnassus*, Freud emphasized a fundamental principle of dream interpretation: the distinction between the dream's underlying thoughts and the form in which those thoughts appeared to the dreamer. Dream thoughts—those ideas which the ego censored from consciousness but which acted nonetheless as the motive force of dreams—defined the dream's latent content, while the images which presented themselves to the dreamer's vision comprised its manifest, surface material. The question of interpretation which confronted Freud at the decisive moment of his career thus resembled that question which faced Warburg when, at a similar point in his early professional life, he explored the intellectual background of Botticelli's paintings. The psychologist who interpreted dreams, just as the art scholar who examined the mystery of Renaissance creativity, endeavored in the first place to answer the question: By what techniques did ideas translate themselves into visual images?

In dreams condensation and displacement served as the most significant means by which thoughts communicated themselves in "pictorial language."[4] Through the process of condensation several ideas, or conflicting strands of thought, attached themselves to a single element within the dream. Mental pictures "constituted 'nodal points' upon which a great number of the dream-thoughts converged."[5] By contrast, the technique of displacement produced not a convergence of ideas but a diversion of thought. An essential piece of the latent dream thoughts became represented by an image of little or no significance within the manifest dream picture, or, conversely, a relatively inconsequential idea received undeserved prominence on the dream's surface. Taking into consideration the techniques of both condensation and displacement Freud concluded that "in the dream-work a psychical force is operating which on the one hand strips the elements which have a high psychical value of their intensity, and on the other hand, *by means of overdetermination*, creates from elements of low psychical value new values, which afterwards find their way into the dream-content. If that is so, *a transference and displacement of psychical intensities* occurs in the process of dream-formation, and it is as a result of these that the difference between the text of the dream-content and that of the dream-thoughts comes about."[6] In a rhythm of destruction and creation, dreams broke down conscious connections and appearances so as to arrange new psychical combinations and compose new mental visions—as the painter Raphael had done in gathering centuries of Greek and Roman philosophers within a single hall, or simultaneously assembling ancient and Renaissance poets in Apollo's presence on Parnassus.

For both Freud and Warburg, determining the techniques by which ideas translated themselves into visual images led to a second, and equally significant, question: How did pictures convey not only an idea, but a sense of living movement? Like the art historian, Freud emphasized that the dynamic qualities of images derived from dramaturgic impulses. Having transformed ideas into pictures, the dreamer incorporated those pictures into a stage setting; as Freud explained in the opening chapter of the dream book, dreams "construct a *situation* out of these images; they represent an event which is actually happening"—in the words of a previous dream theorist, "they 'dramatize' an idea."[7] That theatrical element reflected their chief motive: the dreamer pictured—in disguised or distorted form—a scene in which unconscious wishful impulses realized themselves.

In the dream book's concluding, theoretical chapter Freud returned to the significance of dramaturgy: "Here we have the most general and the most striking psychological characteristic of the process of dreaming: a thought, and as a rule a thought of something that is wished, is objectified in the dream, is represented as a scene, or, as it seems to us, is experienced."[8] Dreams thus produced a sense of movement—or the quality of lived experience—by creating a stage action, or more exactly, by piecing together portions of such actions. What had experienced repression returned in dreams through the medium of mimesis.

To create their stage scenes dreams revived fragments of the past. Indeed, dreaming revealed the close psychological links between image-making, dramatization, and remembrance. Memory developed from the perception of sensory qualities: "A trace is left in our psychical apparatus of the perceptions which impinge upon it. This we may describe as a 'memory-trace'; and to the function relating to it we give the name of 'memory.'"[9] Traces of visual perception formed layers of pictorial fragments within the mind's mnemonic system. Such fragments remained joined by psychological links—unconscious associations between broken images. By a process of psychological regression, ideas or wishes reattached themselves to memory images, drawing from such fragments the pictures with which to express themselves in dreams: "We call it 'regression' when in a dream an idea is turned back into the sensory image from which it was originally derived."[10] Retrieval of sensory images remained the only path of realization for suppressed thoughts and wishes. Such images reappeared with a strong mimetic quality: the dreamer accepted such pictures of absent objects as perceptions of current reality, and entered into imaginary situations as if participating in a scene from life.

The significant role of mimesis in dreaming pointed to the influence exerted by memory fragments themselves, or by fantasies constructed from such fragments: "in dreams too the transformation of thoughts into visual images may be in part the result of the attraction which memories couched in visual form and eager for revival bring to bear upon thoughts cut off from consciousness and struggling to find expression."[11] Unconscious ideas received new life from those memory images, or perceptions, associated with the satisfaction of inward, primal needs. From mental traces of the original experience of satisfaction the unconscious mental system derived the "raw material"[12] from which to build new scenes, or fantasies, of gratification. Further, such fragments of mnemonic images established the links, or paths of association, through which unconscious wishes expressed themselves. By "transferring their own great intensity,"[13] repressed wishes traveled paths of association that linked memory fragments, strengthening the sensory or visual intensity of such fragments and providing those remnants—and the scenes which incorporated them—the psychical energy to enter the dreamer's consciousness. In that process the unconscious wish thereby expressed itself through memory images with which it had no original connection, but to which it had become joined by distant association. Thus the Freudian concept of transference referred from the beginning to assembling the materials and energies for a dramatization: mnemonic fragments offered the material for construction of a scene, while the unconscious wish transmitted the energy with which the stage performance confronted the ego's censorship. The repressed behaved as a dramaturgic force.

Suppressed wishes produced a masked dramatization, communicating themselves only behind the screens—the disguises or distortions—which they acquired in the process of condensation or displacement. Reconfiguration of the wishful image—the construction of a mask—began within the unconscious "primary process."[14] In pursuing immediate gratification, or unimpeded discharge of energy, wishful impulses followed the human being's primal mode of mental activity. Only mobile currents of energy existed within the primary psychical system, in which the mind, obeying the pleasure principle, revived or constructed pictures of fulfillment from fragmented images. Having located memory images through which to transfer and release their energy, unconscious impulses brought mnemonic fragments under the influence of the primary process—in Freud's words, such fragments "become charged with the uninhibited energy from the unconscious which is striving to find an outlet."[15] Yet, before becoming conscious visions, images entered a "secondary process"[16] which inhibited or controlled mental energy, creating in Warburg's phrase, *Denkraum*—reflective space—between impulse and action. Through secondary revision images acquired enough compositional unity to gain the interest and acceptance of the dreamer's ego. Not unlike masks worn within the amphitheater, masks within dreams provided that unified surface necessary for conveying overdetermined and allusive meanings within consciousness.

Dreams thus entered awareness only by a process of mimesis, a process which originated in a psychological regression. Attaching themselves to traces of visual images or scenes, ideas regressively acquired the energy of sensory vividness. Regressive features, however, combined with classical elements from the ancient theater. The rejection of the surface order of existence produced a reality of masked enactments and communications which generated their own sense of living movement and which restored objects that had become lost to consciousness.

III

In dreams, ideas and memory fragments received expression through scenes charged with a sense of motion and intensity. Images appeared as part of a dramatization. Not surprisingly, therefore, even as he concentrated on dream interpretation, Freud began to turn his attention to the meaning of expressive movements. The influence of the unconscious primary process not only entered dreams but also revealed itself in "the transition from preconscious excitation to movement."[17] The unconscious mental energy which animated memory fragments and produced dream images also infused gestures and physical motions. As Freud concluded in *The Interpretation of Dreams*, the art of comedy provided a rich field for the psychological study of expressive motions, not only in the performer but also in the audience: "Evidence, finally, of the increase in activity which becomes necessary when these primary modes of functioning are inhibited is to be found in the fact that we produce a *comic* effect, that is, a surplus of energy which has to be discharged in *laughter, if we allow these modes of thinking to force their way through into consciousness*."[18] Five years after the publication of the dream book, Freud pursued the psychological analysis of comedy and expressive movement in *Jokes and their Relation to the Unconscious*, in which he interpreted comedy as ideational mimetics—the communication of ideas through physical gestures, or through the use of what the mime director and teacher Jacques Lecoq later called the "vocabulary of movement."[19]

Freud's 1905 study focused on jokes and the manipulation of words themselves, before concluding with an examination of the vocabulary of movement. Joke-telling brought to the use of language the techniques of dramatic composition which dreams applied to visual images: the condensation of words, their plastic modification, the utilization of double meanings, and finally, the displacement of meanings through allusion, analogy, and even representation by the opposite. The process of composition itself—the play with words—generated the initial source of enjoyment from joking. Deriving pleasure from the process of mental composition, or from form-giving activity, defined the experience of aesthetic enjoyment. Yet, the pleasure from joking—or the inclination to laughter—emanated from not only the joke's form but also its purpose, or "thought content."[20] Jokes represented hidden acts of rebellion or protest: they carried out aggression, exposed sexual impulses, and questioned accepted mores and popular conventions. In each case, joke-telling aimed at gratifying a repressed desire or instinct. As Freud explained, "to the human psyche all renunciation is exceedingly difficult, and so we find that tendentious jokes provide a means of undoing the renunciation and retrieving what was lost."[21]

To produce pleasure, jokes required an accomplice: an audience. Listeners provided the sanction to express instinctual, hostile, or rebellious inclinations: laughter provided a sign of affirmation. A joke's wordplay ensured such complicity, acting to "bribe the hearer with its yield of pleasure into taking sides with us."[22] The audience therefore appeared not only as a passive recipient of jokes but as an active contributor to the process of joking itself. That process manufactured a pleasurable result through a saving in "psychical expenditure."[23] In giving expression to a repressed thought or aim, jokes spared the expenditure of mental energy on inhibition, releasing that energy as laughter. Wordplay itself elicited enjoyment through a similar saving of energy. The recombination and alteration of common words and phrases, the use of allusions, or the repeating of sounds relieved psychical expenditure by reviving lost associations and links between such words and sounds. Play with language represented the "rediscovery of what is familiar,"[24] and like all types of play, utilized recognition, remembrance, and repetition as mechanisms for gaining pleasure. Such pleasure from language corrupted those forces which opposed the liberation of repressed impulses: the enjoyment of wordplay distractred censorship and undermined the spirit of self-renunciation. Drawing the listener into the pleasures of the past, wordplay corrupted the audience as well. The listener's enjoyment of language allowed him to release mental energy which he had devoted to suppression. Thus, joking became an act of complicity: a form of protest motivated and accomplished by a revival of the past.

An act of hidden complicity: because jokes employed the language and syntax of the unconscious. The suppressed thought or purpose within a joke, just as within a dream, underwent "unconscious revision"[25] before gaining conscious expression. The various techniques of dreams—condensation, abbreviation, double meaning, allusion, representation by the opposite—appeared also in jokes. In the same sense that fragments of images rearranged themselves through unconscious links into a dream composition, so the language of joking proved to be self-creative. In Vienna at the turn of the century, the satirist Karl Kraus proclaimed the spontaneous creativity of language and desperately campaigned against modern cultural forces which eroded that creativity. Kraus recognized no allies in his crusade but perceived in Freud's early theory a position in some measure similar to his own, acknowledging that commonality with characteristic Krausian irony: "F. has demonstrated the relationship between jokes and dreams. It is not his fault, if among the treasures which he has extracted from the unconscious, now and again a sapphire turns up."[26]

The rechanneling of unconscious energy and the psychological recovery of what had been lost occurred not only in wordplay and dream images but also in comedic movements and gestures. Comedy originated in ideational mimetics, or the process by which a human being seeking to convey an idea "represents its subject-matter in his expressive movements."[27] Physical expressiveness, however, did not limit itself to the purpose of communication: Freud observed that "these mimetics exist, even with less liveliness, quite apart from any communication, that they occur as well when the subject is forming an idea of something for his own private benefit and is thinking of something pictorially, and that he then expresses 'large' and 'small' in his own body just as he does in speech, at all events by a change in the innervation of his features and sense organs."[28] Further, the mimetic representation of thoughts appeared not only as the physical expression of mental images but also as the somatic tension which commonly accompanied intellectual concentration and conceptualization. Freud defended "the view that to the 'expression of the emotions,' which is well known as the physical concomitant of mental processes, there should be added the 'expression of the ideational content.' "[29] Through a study of the comic the psychoanalyst began to develop a psychology of expressive movement, which several years later he applied to an understanding of ritual behavior and dramatic enactments.[30]

Comedy in fact derived from primal, mimic behavior, or pantomime, the purest form of expressive motion. The comic mime introduced "exaggerated expressive movements"[31] into his stage behavior and gestures, all to the pleasure of audiences, who enjoyed comparing the comic actor's excessive stage motions to their own nonstage, self-contained actions. Such comparison required that the observer translate the actor's movements into an imitative idea or inward model.

Immediate understanding of an action—or rather of the energy required to produce that action—derived from physical imitation. The effort to imitate inspired perception, as Freud concluded: "An impulsion of this kind to imitation is undoubtedly present in perceptions of movements."[32] The energy of imitation thus channeled itself into both movement and thought. Specifically, the mental energy expended on forming the idea of an act reflected the energy which belonged to the act itself: expenditure on a motion translated into the mental expenditure required to preserve the idea of that motion. The ideas which we constructed of our own and others' actions thus acquired psychological intensity from the tendency to re-create those actions inwardly—to produce mental likenesses of them. Those likenesses, and the energy which attached to them, survived as fragments of memory. The observer of a comic action did not need to reproduce that action physically in order to understand it and compare it to his own; rather, he formed a conception of the act through "memory-traces of expenditures on similar movements."[33]

By producing a mental likeness of the comedian's movement, the observer created an identity between himself and the comic performer. Identification allowed the observer to imagine himself in the situation of the performer, imitating in thought the actor's exaggerated movement. At the same time, he called to mind the energy necessary in his own experience to accomplish the purpose of the act; speaking for the observer, Freud explained: "I disregard the person whom I am observing and behave as though I myself wanted to reach the aim of the movement."[34] Thus, through psychological simulation the observer inwardly reproduced both the psychical energy which attached to the idea of an exaggerated, comic movement and that energy which belonged to an appropriate, restricted motion. The quantity of mental energy in excess of that needed to understand and preserve an accurate idea of the spectator's original, limited action released itself in the audience as laughter and enjoyment of the performance. Pleasure from comedy therefore derived from a process by which observers inwardly reenacted two sets of movements—those of the comic actor and those which they recovered from their own pasts.

Pantomime provided the key to explaining caricature or parody. In one regard, caricature—the exaggerated emphasis on unique gestures or physical features—represented a continuation of miming, and the irreverence of such mimic depictions opened new sources of enjoyment. The idea of the sublime, or the attitude of reverence itself, demanded in human beings an increased psychical expenditure. By creating a link between a revered being and its irreverent likeness the caricaturist reduced the amount of mental energy expended on an object previously held in awe and released the remaining, unnecessary quantity as comic pleasure. Thus did the art of caricature manipulate the psychological identity between a grimacing figure and one displaying grace.

From the study of dream images Freud had moved to the analysis of wordplay and the physical vocabulary of movement, demonstrating how the techniques of image-making, language, and expressive movement possessed various dramaturgic qualities. In dream compositions, mental pictures conveyed the sense of a living reality by arranging themselves within a stage scene or sequence. Through such dramatizations, dreams reflected the suppressed striving to repeat a lost experience of fulfillment.

Jokes, on the other hand, transformed their own raw material—the material of language—into play, and thus re-created an activity which served as an early source of enjoyment. Whereas dream images produced the conviction of a living reality through the visualization of a dramatic scene, jokes drew the listener into their world through the revival of play acting. Drawing on elements of both theater and children's play, expressive movements and gestures centered on manufacturing an identity between actor and observer. The physical act of imitating another's movements served as the primal mode of perception and identification. Imitation, however, also occurred in thought. Observing or conceptualizing an action required an expenditure of mental energy which corresponded to the energy which had been devoted to the action itself. Observers psychologically identified with an actor by expending energy on recalling the actor's movements, or on reproducing them in thought. Ideation became a mode of reenacting movements, an indication that thought itself originated as a mimic endeavor. Expressive movement thereby mobilized a primordial psychology of identification: the identity between an observer and comic actor became so complete as to remove momentarily the psychological boundaries between the self and other.

In adopting a dynamic and dramaturgic approach to the interpretation of dream images and expressive movement Freud evidenced a perspective similar to that of Warburg. Both researchers perceived in pictures and gestures the fragments of a stage action. Not surprisingly, Freud, like the Renaissance scholar, began his own explorations of art and the rebirth of the ancient past by interpreting an image of movement—the sculpted image of Gradiva, whose careful, gentle step recalled the dancelike movements of Botticelli's Graces.

IV

In the summer of 1906, the year following the publication of the joke book, Freud wrote his analysis of Wilhelm Jensen's short story, "Gradiva: A Pompeian Fantasy." Freud's work—*Delusions and Dreams in Jensen's "Gradiva"*—appeared in print in May 1907. Jensen's story provided Freud with the opportunity to demonstrate how a creative writer—independently of any Freudian influence—understood in a psychoanalytic sense the significance of dreams and the nature of therapeutic cures. Dreaming, Freud wrote, remained a foreign matter to ordinary psychological science, for which, "dreams are comparable only to twitchings, not to expressive movements, of the mind."[35] In contending that dreams had comprehensible meanings, the psychoanalyst declared himself "a partisan of antiquity and superstition"[36]—a declaration to which Aby Warburg, the student of ancient mysteries and astrological symbols, might also have added his name. To understand Gradiva's image required, however, that researchers interpret not only the fictional hero's dreams, but also Gradiva's own expressive gestures.

Jensen's story began when the protagonist, Norbert Hanold—an archeologist by profession—encountered in a Rome museum an ancient bas relief of a young woman (Figure 13). Although the woman's pose resembled classical images of goddesses or nymphs, the archeologist—unlike Freud—did not perceive in her a figure from mythology. Jensen described the sculpted figure as Hanold observed her:

> In no way did she remind one of the numerous extant bas-reliefs of a Venus, a Diana, or other Olympian goddess, and equally little of a Psyche or nymph. In her was embodied something humanly commonplace—not in a bad sense—to a degree a sense of present time, as if the artist, instead of making a pencil sketch of her on a sheet of paper, as is done in our day, had fixed her in a clay model quickly, from life, as she passed on the street, a tall, slight figure, whose soft, wavy hair a folded kerchief almost completely bound. Her rather slender face was not at all dazzling, and the desire to produce such effect was obviously equally foreign to her; in the delicately formed features was expressed a nonchalant equanimity in regard to what was occurring about her; her eye, which gazed calmly ahead, bespoke absolutely unimpaired powers of vision and thoughts quietly withdrawn.[37]

The sculptor conveyed her living qualities chiefly through the tender but secure motion of her step: "So the young woman was fascinating, not at all because of plastic beauty of form, but because she possessed something rare in antique sculpture—a realistic, simple, maidenly grace which gave the impression of imparting life to the relief. This was effected chiefly by the movement represented in the picture. . . . This movement produced a double impression of exceptional agility and of confident composure, and the flight-like poise, combined with a firm step, lent her the peculiar grace."[38] Having been so taken with the sculpture, the archeologist felt compelled to choose a name for it: "he had called it to himself Gradiva, 'the girl splendid in walking.' "[39]

The first encounter with the ancient sculpture led the archeologist to construct for himself a more detailed mental picture of Gradiva and her world. Concluding that the figure in the relief had lived in Pompeii, he imagined the young woman moving through its marketplace and pillared streets. Like a Renaissance humanist questing after the Greek original of a Roman copy, Hanold further decided that her ancestors must have belonged to those ancient Greeks who had settled in southern Italy. Having thus manufactured a scene in which to place Gradiva, and devised for her a Greek origin, the ancient scholar preoccupied himself with another question—"whether the artist had reproduced Gradiva's manner of walking from life."[40] He made a study of contemporary women in the act of walking but found none who re-created Gradiva's pose. As a result, his researches produced in him a mixed feeling of disturbance and sadness: "his observations caused him annoyance, for he found the vertical position of the lingering foot beautiful, and regretted that it had been created by the imagination or arbitrary act of the sculptor and did not correspond to reality."[41] While the archeologist recognized in the image of Gradiva a quality of living movement, he admitted that the figure did not copy reality, an admission which produced in him a sense of inward loss.

Having unsuccessfully sought a model of Gradiva in his own world, Hanold dreamt that he found himself in Pompeii in the year A.D. 79, on the day of its destruction beneath Vesuvius, and there he finally saw Gradiva herself before she perished with her city. The vision intensified his feeling of deprivation, which, however, became replaced on the morning following the dream by a conviction that he momentarily observed Gradiva walking in his own street. The dream thus marked a transition between Hanold's mental pictures of the sculpted figure and his delusions about Gradiva's actual presence. Not long after the experience of the dream and delusion, the archeologist developed a longing for travel,

13. *Gradiva* relief. Museo Chiaramonti, Vatican Museums. Photo: Scala/Art Resource, New York.

"a nameless feeling"[42] which he finally justified to himself by the need to examine certain Roman statues. Such justification came naturally to an ancient scholar for whom the present appeared "only in the most shadowy way," and for whom "marble and bronze were not dead, but rather the only really vital thing which expressed the purpose and value of human life."[43] The sudden, unprepared decision to travel led Hanold on a journey to Rome, from where his restlessness impelled him to Naples, and finally to the ancient remains of Pompeii.

In Pompeii Hanold's delusions became such that the ghost of Gradiva seemed to appear before him, and even converse with him at midday among the city's ruins. The scholar's illness had developed to its crisis point: from that moment began his recovery. In the apparition Hanold slowly recognized the original model of Gradiva from his own experience, and his true midday companion: his brief childhood love, Zoe Bertgang, who resided on his home street, and whom he had ignored for years. A traveler herself in Pompeii, Zoe Bertgang—whose name derived from the Greek word for 'life' and the German for 'brightly walking'—gradually brought Hanold to relinquish his delusions, to reenter the world of the present, and most important, to rediscover his love for her.

Freud's study gave careful attention to the process of recovery, during which Hanold, under Zoe Bertgang's guidance, slowly perceived the links not only between Gradiva and his childhood love but also between elements of his delusions and early experiences which he had long forgotten—experiences which had nonetheless remained buried in deeper strata of his mind. When early erotic feelings, which he had suppressed from thought, reemerged to consciousness his last illusions dissolved themselves. The dream of Pompeii—only the first of similarly significant dreams in the story—had not only led Hanold to the point of crisis but also indicated its resolution: the scene of the archeologist encountering Gradiva during Pompeii's final hours retranslated and dramatized his unconscious knowledge that Zoe Bertgang—Gradiva's living model— dwelled near to him in the present, knowledge which at that time he continued to suppress.

In stressing the archeologist's encounter with the ancient sculpture of Gradiva, and his sudden, at first inexplicable determination to visit the famous ruins of Pompeii, Jensen's story centered on that theme which we initially met in Warburg and have now followed to Freud: the impact of an expressive movement in a visual image from the past. Warburg originally explored that problem in the figures of Botticelli's nymphs, to whom Gradiva—in her graceful movement, and despite Hanold's disclaimers—bears justifiable comparison. Her pose, for example, resembles that of the female figure on the extreme right in Filippino Lippi's drawing, *Birth of Venus* (Figure 14). Fritz Saxl described that drawing, which he labeled, "Three Nymphs," as an image which typified the classical revival of the early Renaissance.[44] In the 1912 postscript to his study of Jensen's story, Freud himself linked the image of Gradiva directly to the classical figures which appeared in Renaissance paintings. Housed in the Vatican collection, the actual Gradiva sculpture had belonged to an ancient Roman copy of a relief of Greek origin which depicted the three Horae—goddesses of the seasons and divine embodiments of the natural cycle of life, death, and rebirth. One of the Horae survived as Gradiva.[45]

In Jensen's story the archeologist's urge to explain the sense of movement which animated Gradiva's image ultimately led to a process of rebirth resembling that which Warburg had identified in Botticelli: the devotee of antiquity, already familiar with its marble survivals, constructed his own mental scenes from remnants of the ancient world, thereby confronting that world in a more immediate, and finally more deeply disruptive way. Among the ancient ruins a delusional reality took hold of Hanold's ego: to the once sober-minded archeologist the young woman in the sculpture seemed to have returned to life, not in a work of art, but as a revenant of antiquity. The search for Gradiva in the fragments of Pompeii's past threatened a loss of self.

In the revival of antiquity as described in Jensen's fictional work Freud too found a process which threatened a shattering of the ego. Confronting an ancient image which stirred in him a repressed vision, the scholarly ascetic projected onto the sculpture an overwhelming sense of life and movement. The experienced archeologist applied a lifelong, professional remedy, seeking control over his projections by journeying to Rome, Naples, and ultimately to Pompeii, there to approach the ancient

14. Filippino Lippi, *Birth of Venus*. JBS 41 verso. Oxford, Christ Church Picture Gallery. Photo: The Governing Body, Christ Church, Oxford.

past as a stone ruin and object of cold criticism. Yet, as the French philosopher and literary critic, Sarah Kofman wrote of Hanold, "it is this critical faculty that leads him, by an inevitable psychic process, to crisis point."[46] Sacrificing itself to a world of bronze and marble, the ego submits to a delusional reality. The archeologist's effort to repicture Gradiva's life and to renew contact with her former world, however, allowed the suppressed image to acquire consciousness, until at last Hanold recognized the actual model of Gradiva. The ancient scholar's behavior demonstrated in a striking manner that principle which Freud placed at the center of both mental and cultural science: "the instrument of repression . . . becomes the vehicle for the return."[47]

The development of the archeologist's delusion marked the gradual resurfacing of the scholar's unconscious reminiscences. Indeed, the visions which took hold of Hanold represented "transformed memories."[48] The image of Gradiva's movement reanimated the memory of Zoe Bertgang's graceful step. Hanold's dream of being with Gradiva at the destruction of Pompeii transposed into dream imagery his unconscious recollection that his early—and only—love in fact resided near to him in the present. In Pompeii itself, at the most extreme stage of his delusion, the repressed emerged into full consciousness, and the archeologist finally recognized not a female spirit resurrected from antiquity but a woman of flesh and blood from his own past: "A return like this of what has been repressed is to be expected with particular regularity when a person's erotic feelings are attached to the repressed impressions—when his erotic life has been attacked by repression."[49] The image of the young woman walking had led him into a delusional state but had also restored to him his memory and his reality, enabling a modern rebirth of Eros.

The progress of the archeologist's delusion and the process of return traveled a path which led from visualization to drama. An artwork initially conveyed to Hanold an impression of immediacy and movement. Under the powerful influence of that impression, the scholarly observer sought to produce his own mental image of the figure. Attempting to summon the artist's original vision, he searched for models of Gradiva's pose and compared his own observations to the sculptor's work. In the effort to reconceive Gradiva and to identify with the sculptor, the repressed memory emerged only faintly in imagination, as Hanold ultimately decided that Gradiva represented an entirely artistic invention. The return of the repressed became complete only when Hanold's delusions entered their final, dramaturgic phase during his archeological tour of southern Italy. Having transferred his feelings of loss and regret onto an inexpressible need for travel, the archeologist sought refuge from the present in the relics of Pompeii's ancient past. There he observed Gradiva's movements and gestures enacted before him. No longer did she appear to him as a figure of sculpture or imagination but as a revenant from the ancient world who moved once more on the stage of the living. Only when his delusion reached that moment of dramatization did he recognize in the female tourist in Pompeii Gradiva's actual model. What Hanold perceived as the reborn spirit of Gradiva proved to be a reenactment from his own past—in Kofman's words, "a drama played out on a double scene."[50] The acting out of what he had lost occurred only within the precincts of ancient Pompeii, which embodied both the burial of the past and its restoration: "Finally, his phantasy transported her to Pompeii, not 'because her quiet, calm nature seemed to demand it,' but because no other or better analogy could be found in his science for his remarkable state, in which he became aware of his memories of his childhood friendship through obscure channels of information. Once he had made his own childhood coincide with the classical past (which it was so easy for him to do), there was a perfect similarity between the burial of Pompeii—the disappearance of the past combined with its preservation—and repression, of which he possessed a knowledge through what might be described as 'endopsychic' perception."[51] The image of Gradiva revived personal memories, but the rediscovery of the ancient past in Italy dramatized them. Without that dramatization—without the journey to Pompeii through which Hanold physically enacted and brought to its completion the mental process of return—the archeologist could not have been freed of his delusions.

As with his interpretation of dreams and comedy, Freud's study of Gradiva connected mental images and expressive movements to a process of dramatic reenactment. By enacting a portion of the original sculptor's creative process and producing his own mental image of Gradiva, Hanold achieved a more convincing projection of the absent object, and of the feelings associated with her. That projection ultimately assumed a dramaturgic existence, toward which Hanold redirected the attitude and behavior which he once had applied to the figure from childhood. Ultimately, the archeologist fully simulated the inward reemergence of the past which his observation of Gradiva's image had initiated by sojourning among the surviving remnants of antiquity in Italy.

The problem of mimesis, as much as the novelist's concern with dreams and cures, drew Freud's interest to Jensen's story, in which each effort at reimagination, each attempt at mental or visual reconstruction led to a dramatic enactment of fragments from the past. In Freud's interpretation, those fragments belonged to Hanold's personal history. For Warburg, the rebirth of the past occurred also as an artistic and historical process, a perspective which Freud finally adopted in the years immediately following the publication of the Gradiva study. Before the onset of the First World War Freud explored image-making and dramatic enactment in both art and history, doing so through his own studies of Renaissance art and primal ritual.

V

In December 1907, the year in which his Gradiva study appeared, Freud delivered a lecture within a series organized by Hugo Heller, the Viennese publisher, bookseller, and member of the Vienna Psychoanalytic Society. Published the following year under the title "Creative Writers and Day-Dreaming," the lecture described how the creative process brought about a restoration of the past. Like Warburg, Freud argued that to understand a work of art required that one reconstruct the process by which the artist manufactured a mental image of his work. That inward image not only transmitted to the artwork a quality of motion but also restored models from the past. As Freud's lecture explained, early in life inventive imagination expressed itself in play, through which a child "creates a world of his own, or, rather, re-arranges the things of his world in a new way which pleases him."[52] With the years, the manufacture of fantasies—or the activity of daydreaming—succeeded the dramaturgic construction of worlds through play. Yet, as the psychoanalyst explained to his listeners: "Actually, we never give anything up; we only exchange one thing for another. What appears to be a renunciation is really the formation of a substitute or surrogate."[53] Fantasizing thus served as a mental imitation of— or psychological surrogate for—the activity of play, a process of inward reenactment similar to the spectator's mental re-creation of a comedian's movements.

Fantasy invention combined material from the present with fragments of memory to construct a scene which portrayed the fulfillment of a wish. That psychological formula also elucidated the creative process: "A strong experience in the present awakens in the creative writer a memory of an earlier experience (usually belonging to his childhood) from which there now proceeds a wish which finds its fulfilment in the creative work."[54] The reemergence of a fragment of the past impelled the writer to a more thorough, if still indirect, restoration of what had become lost to consciousness. Indeed, as a reenactment of playful activity, creative writing itself remained close to remnants of the past: summarizing his theory of creativity, Freud noted that "the stress it lays on childhood memories in the writer's life—a stress which may perhaps seem puzzling—is ultimately derived from the assumption that a piece of creative writing, like a daydream, is a continuation of, and a substitute for, what was once the play of childhood."[55] The reader's enjoyment of creative works derived at least in some measure from participation in that reenactment, or play acting, just as the audience to a joke experienced pleasure from mere wordplay. As did the wordplay in jokes, the form in which writers presented their creative works acted as a bribe "offered to us so as to make possible the release of still greater pleasure arising from deeper psychical sources."[56] Enjoyment of the formal, or aesthetic, qualities of a creative work led the audience to share further in the world of the writer's invention—in his own stage activity—and so find an equivalent for the dramaturgic outlet of their own suppressed impulses.

Although his presentation to Heller's literary audience concerned itself specifically with products of the writer's imagination, Freud first applied the creative formula which he introduced in the lecture to an understanding of the supreme exemplar of Renaissance painting. Freud's psychoanalytic biography of Leonardo da Vinci, published in 1910, examined Leonardo's paintings for the restoration of memory fragments. Leonardo's artwork, however, also possessed dramaturgic elements, which Freud traced first to the subtle gesture of the Mona Lisa del Giocondo's smile, and which he explored more extensively within the painter's *Virgin and Child and St. Anne* in the Louvre. As in the case of Warburg's Renaissance studies, Freud's analysis of Leonardo's painting moved from interpreting an expressive movement to delineating a type of stage action.

Agreeing with generations of art critics and historians, Freud perceived in Mona Lisa's mysterious and quiet gesture of smiling the expression of conflicting tendencies: specifically, "the contrast between reserve and seduction, and between the most devoted tenderness and a sensuality that is ruthlessly demanding."[57] Mona Lisa had revived within Leonardo the memory of his natural mother, with whom he had shared only his first years of life, and who had devoted to her infant son, and sought from him, an especially affectionate and intimate love. The smile, and the erotic emotions which it embodied, belonged originally to Leonardo's mother and appeared in the portrait as a gesture which recalled an absent world. The influence of that memory trace, and the unconscious feelings which attached to it, received richer dramaturgic expression in the painting of the *Virgin and Child and St. Anne* (Figure 15). In that artwork Leonardo constructed a scene which dramatized his early childhood experiences and his relationships to his mother and stepmother. A youthful Mary extended her arms with protective care to her infant, while St. Anne, seemingly near to her daughter's age, lovingly observed the mother with her child. The painting produced the fragment of a stage action, an image which created in the figure of Mary the woman whom Leonardo's father married and who looked after Leonardo throughout most of his childhood, and in St. Anne, the natural mother toward whom he directed his first erotic impulses. The two figures shared with Mona Lisa that smile which for the painter embodied the essence of both sensual love and spiritual adoration. As Paul Ricoeur described, for Leonardo that essence reduced itself to a sense of the presence of absent objects—a dramaturgic sense. Whereas Ricoeur saw in Leonardo's art the creation of new objects in response to an

15. Leonardo da Vinci, *Virgin and Child and St. Anne*. Paris, Musée de Louvre.
Photo: Alinari/Art Resource, New York.

inward absence, Freud perceived the simulation of distant figures within a stage scene.[58]

The fragments of the past which Renaissance painters incorporated into their works revived suppressed instinctual forces: Italian Renaissance art transformed those primeval tendencies into exalted expressions. For both Warburg and Freud the artistic sublimation of forces from the primitive past defined both the highest achievement of the Italian Renaissance and its most tenuous accomplishment. Failed sublimation threatened the artist with a splitting of the self. According to Warburg, Renaissance painters who revived images of pagan antiquity in their works risked losing their spiritual identities to the resurgence of primitive emotions. In Freud's biography of Leonardo, the artist fell prey to the opposite extreme: the repression which governed his erotic life took possession of his painting. Only occasionally thereafter did the unrecognized return of memory traces provide an inspiration to the painter's creative genius. Ultimately, the split within Leonardo caused his scientific interests completely to submerge his artistic pursuits. In that regard Leonardo's tragedy typified what Freud perceived as the defining conflict of Renaissance civilization, "an age which saw a struggle between sensuality without restraint and gloomy asceticism."[59] Yet, in the moments of unrivaled artistic triumph, Leonardo neither shunned the world of the senses nor surrendered to pagan images but constructed from the fragmentary, primal material of his past, visions of mysteriously balanced forces.

Freud's study of Renaissance visual arts included not only Leonardo's painting but also Michelangelo's sculpture of Moses, on which the psychoanalyst had been meditating since his first visit to Rome in 1901 (Figure 16). On that journey Freud wrote to his wife that he had visited the Church of San Pietro in Vincoli, the location of Michelangelo's statue.[60] On further trips to Italy he returned to the church, finally determining during his visit in 1912 to compose an essay on the subject of the statue. From Rome he informed his wife of the decision, writing that "every day I pay a visit to Moses in S. Pietro in Vincoli, on whom I may perhaps write a few words."[61] Freud's essay, "The Moses of Michelangelo," which appeared in *Imago* in 1914, revealed an aim similar to that of Warburg's early studies: to find the artist's mental vision and intellectual purpose from "the residue of a movement."[62] James Fenton noted Freud's interest in the problem of the sculpture's mimetic effect, his fascination, as in the analysis of Jensen's Gradiva, with "the idea that a marble sculpture might come to life."[63] As Fenton described, the psychoanalyst imagined that he could unravel the mysteries of the figure of Moses "if he came cautiously upon the statue, and seized upon its living self."[64]

To understand Michelangelo's vision and Moses' living quality, Freud examined the sculptor's dramaturgic technique, but in contrast to the case of Leonardo, he sought within the statue neither a portion of memory nor the restoration of an object. Rather, the psychoanalyst attempted to reconstruct the dramatic action of which the moment depicted by Michelangelo formed a part. In Michelangelo's sculpture, Moses appeared seated, his left foot raised, his right arm and hand pressed tightly against the Tablets of Law, and the fingers of his right hand entangled in his beard. Freud departed from earlier interpreters who viewed the sculpture either as a representation of the instant at which Moses began to rise in anger against his unrighteous followers, or as a symbolic embodiment of the prophet's moral passion and unconquerable will. Referring to the details of the positions of the statue's arm, fingers, and foot, Freud argued instead that Michelangelo sculpted Moses in the act of recovering his rage and redirecting it inward. By controlling both his instinctive anger, and the impulsive movement which resulted from it, Moses demonstrated his devotion to the law inscribed on the Tablets, and the inward sacrifice it required of him. To support his interpretation Freud included with the essay two drawings which portrayed the figure of Moses in a sequence of movements leading to the moment preserved in the sculpture. Michelangelo incorporated remnants of the full dramatic sequence into the sculpted image of the lawgiver: "The lines of the face reflect the feelings which have won the ascendancy; the middle of the figure shows the traces of suppressed movement; and the foot still retains the attitude of the projected action."[65]

Similar to the efforts of both Warburg and Loewy, Freud's essay endeavored to reproduce the artist's mental picture of his creation.[66] In the case of Michelangelo's Moses, Freud sought to illuminate that internal vision, and the intention behind it, by reconstructing the scene in

16. Michelangelo, *Moses.* Rome, San Pietro in Vincoli. Photo: Foto Marburg/Art Resource, New York.

which the artist imagined the Jewish prophet. That scene removed Moses from his Biblical context and situated him within a Renaissance drama. Michelangelo's Moses experienced the Renaissance struggle which Warburg had found projected onto the artwork of the Sassetti chapel: the conflict between a life of action and a life of contemplation, between a drive to master the outer world and an urge to withdraw inward. According to Freud, the artist intended through the sculpture of the lawgiver to delineate a figure who in a moment of crisis subordinated his action to the demands of thought and restrained his anger in submission to a higher law. Freud acknowledged that Michelangelo's intention in sculpting Moses necessarily remained difficult to reach, but even to glimpse that intention required that the observer perceive the art object as part of a dramaturgic reenactment.

In 1912, the year in which he decided to publish his analysis of Michelangelo's sculpture, Freud directed his attention as well to the problem with which Warburg had begun his career as an art historian: the appearance of the ancient Graces in Renaissance culture. Whereas Warburg first interpreted images of the Graces in the figures of Botticelli's nymphs, Freud turned to their representation on Shakespeare's stage. In a letter to Sándor Ferenczi in June 1912, the psychoanalyst first communicated his ideas on the subject, and in the following year, published them in *Imago* in an essay entitled, "The Theme of the Three Caskets."[67]

The scene from *The Merchant of Venice* in which Portia's suitors must choose correctly between three caskets in order to win her hand provided the starting point of Freud's reflections. Only one suitor chooses wisely, selecting the lead casket, which holds Portia's picture. Although transformed, the scene retained its kinship to ancient legends in which a man confronts a choice between three women, such as that which Paris faced in judging the beauty of Aphrodite, the goddess of love, against that of her two rivals. Shakespeare himself introduced the pagan theme not only into *The Merchant of Venice*, but also into the tragedy of *King Lear*— and transformed it once again. Lear determines to divide his lands among his three daughters but denies a portion to the most devoted of the three, Cordelia, because she declines to put her love into words. In mythology and legend, muteness signified the silent force of death. In myths based upon a choice between three women, the attribute of silence demonstrated the presence of the goddess of death in one of the female figures: "But if the third of the sisters is the Goddess of Death, the sisters are known to us. They are the Fates, the Moerae, the Parcae or the Norns, the third of whom is called Atropos, the inexorable."[68]

The ancient Greek conception of the Fates as three sister-goddesses derived, Freud wrote, from their kinship in mythology to the Graces—the three companions of Aphrodite—and to the three Horae. The figures of the Horae, who originated as goddesses of vegetation and the cycle of the seasons, "became the guardians of natural law and of the divine Order which causes the same thing to recur in Nature in an unalterable sequence."[69] The three Moerae came to represent the fatality of law in human existence, ensuring "the necessary ordering of human life as inexorably as do the Horae over the regular order of nature."[70] In ancient legends which confronted men with a choice between three women, human wishful impulses transfigured the goddess of death—who imposed her law remorselessly upon humankind—into a deeply desired object of tenderness and love. That transformation, which remodeled a figure of fate into an object of desire, recalled the primitive union between goddesses of death and destruction, and goddesses of love and fertility—an ancient identification which applied to the earliest conceptions of the Greek Aphrodite. Thus, in the legendary motif of choice, "the replacement by a wishful opposite . . . harks back to a primaeval identity."[71]

In *King Lear*, Shakespeare worked his own transformation of the ancient myth of choice, while simultaneously restoring a portion of its primal meaning. Lear's tragedy culminated with his final entrance on stage—a broken man, enraged and no longer self-deceiving, cradling in his arms the lifeless body of Cordelia, whose graciousness, youth, and untimely fate cannot but remind us of the vision of Simonetta dei Vespucci in Botticelli's *Primavera*. The king's youngest daughter—the true representative of love within the drama—at last appears as a figure of death in whom Lear now recognizes his own unavoidable destiny. That reappearance of the primordial, mythic object during Lear's final stage action explained the play's dramatic impact: "It is by means of this reduction of the distortion, this partial return to the original, that the dramatist achieves his more profound effect upon us."[72]

The figure of Cordelia emerged on stage as the final Renaissance recreation of the Graces, a revenant of the divine nymphs who accompanied Venus and celebrated the seasonal restoration of life. The pagan Graces, however, not only granted a vision of sublime love and earthly renewal but also, as Warburg warned, harbored a reminder of the dissolution of the self and final return to nature. Shakespeare's Cordelia shared that dual essence. In her character Shakespeare not only brought to culmination the Renaissance revival of classical images but simultaneously evoked a figure from primal consciousness. Her stage action revealed itself as an overdetermined process: the enactment of her presence in the theater masked the revival of a more distant, primitive object. That primeval figure embodied the muteness of the laws of nature and the silent turnings of fate. Thus Cordelia—the Shakespearean Grace—expressed her deepest impulses not in words but instead in the vocabulary of movement.[73]

VI

As with Warburg's studies of painting, Freud's Renaissance essays of 1910 to 1914 combined an interest in expressive movement with an exploration of the primal content of classical revivals. For Freud, as for Warburg, the delineation of movement and the composition of dramatic scenes—on canvas and on stage—regenerated primordial emotions and beliefs. The psychical energy which belonged to an ancient action infused the ideas or images of that act. The construction of mental pictures and visual images therefore served to a significant degree as a reenactment.

During the years in which he wrote his studies of Renaissance culture, Freud conceived and published his theory of the primeval origins of human civilization. In 1912 and 1913, the essays expounding that theory appeared in Vienna's *Imago*; the journal's publisher, Hugo Heller issued them in a single book volume before the end of 1913 under the title, *Totem and Taboo*. The essays explored the historical, as well as the emotional and psychological content of expressive movement. Just as traces of pagan antiquity surfaced in Renaissance images, fragments of civilization's primal beginnings survived in the motions and scenarios of ritual enactments.

The journal *Imago* indicated in its title a connection which Viennese psychoanalysts perceived between image-making and ritual activity. Hanns Sachs, a founding editor of the journal and a member of the Vienna Psychoanalytic Society, suggested the title from the novel by Carl Spitteler of the same name. In Sachs's explanation, the term *imago* referred to an unconscious mental image constructed from memory traces. Such an image served as a model projected not only onto artistic creations but also onto figures in the real world.[74] In two essays published in 1912 Freud employed the concept of imago to explain the phenomenon of transference in psychoanalytic therapy and the choice of love object in ordinary life. In therapy a patient projected onto the figure of the analyst an unconscious, prototypical image, and enacted toward the analyst the feelings and reactions which applied to that prototype.[75] Similar prototypes, or models, influenced an individual's choice of love object.[76] In both instances, imago described an unconscious model composed of memory fragments and of the emotions belonging to them—a mental image such as that which determined the archeologist's reaction to Gradiva and Leonardo's response to the figure of Mona Lisa del Giocondo. As with dream symbols, the imago did not represent an abstraction or uniform type, but rather a model with rich mnemonic and emotional textures. Further, as demonstrated by the phenomenon of transference, the unconscious exemplar expressed itself not only through projection onto an external figure or creative work but also through reenactment and dramatization.[77] In Freud's theory of the origins of civilization ritual performance represented the collective enactment of an imago from the past, reviving primal memories and impulses, and reproducing fragments of historical reactions and events.

In *Totem and Taboo* Freud examined the system of primitive animism to demonstrate the religious and social significance of externalized imagos. The animistic worldview recognized the presence of independent spirits throughout creation and the existence of souls in all natural objects, tracing causation in nature to the action of such spirits or souls. Spirits originated as external projections of thoughts and impulses. The animistic system, however, represented significantly more than a vast collection of individual projections. In its completeness and coherence it provided the first full image of the human psychical system: "primitive man transposed the structural conditions of his own mind into the external world."[78] Just as Jensen's archeologist outwardly demonstrated through his renewed interest in Pompeii the process of repression of which he was inwardly—or endopsychically—aware, early humanity gave external representation to the human mental system which it understood through similar "endopsychic perception."[79] The first intellectual worldview thus came into being as an intricate picture of inward psychical reality fastened onto nature.

That vision of realty provided a scenario within which individuals interpreted and determined their actions. Spiritualized figures—the precursors of gods and of mythic heroes—entered experience as figures who demanded human reaction, or whom individuals sought to influence through their own acts. In the modern world artistic creation survived through its own animistic system, or magical projection of inward needs and wishes: "Only in art does it still happen that a man who is consumed by desires performs something resembling the accomplishment of those desires and that what he does in play produces emotional effects—thanks to artistic illusion—just as though it were something real."[80] The animistic mentality survived as well within modern audiences, who responded to idealized images or illusions as if they possessed actual existence.

In its earliest phase the animistic system built upon remembrances. Human beings originally created spirits as projections of their thoughts and feelings toward the dead: "It might be said that in the last analysis the 'spirit' of persons or things comes down to their capacity to be remembered and imagined after perception of them has ceased."[81] Such creations enabled primitive mourners to control disruptive, ambivalent emotions. Lamentation externalized hostile feelings toward the dead in the form of aggressive, dangerous spirits demanding propitiation: the souls of absent figures remained alive and present, but as objects of fear. The sense of the spirit's immediate nearness and the oppressive fear of its hostility faded with the process of grieving, ultimately replaced by an attitude of reverence toward the souls of ancestors. The animistic worldview, however, continued to nurture a conviction in the existence of vengeful spirits, who derived from overdetermined, unconscious models, and entered awareness as projected fragments of such models.

Memory fragments survived not only in animistic projections but also in ceremonial enactments. Primitive ritual performances re-created portions of events from the most distant period of civilization, and the traces of primal rites which reappeared in the ceremonies of pagan antiquity thus restored decaying but genuine remnants of the earliest historical occurrences. Freud accepted the conclusion reached by biblical scholar and anthropologist William Robertson Smith that rites of sacrifice found within late antiquity derived from the primeval celebration of the totem meal: "The oldest form of sacrifice, then, older than the use of fire or the knowledge of agriculture, was the sacrifice of animals, whose flesh and blood were enjoyed in common by the god and his worshippers. It was essential that each one of the participants should have his share of the meal."[82] The primeval community offered as the sacrificial victim its own totem animal, the figure through which the collectivity defined its identity and unity: "the sacrificing community, the god and the sacrificial animal were of the same blood and members of one clan."[83]

The totem feast ceremonially reenacted the event which brought civilization into being—the slaying of the primal father and the creation of a community of brothers. Prior to the appearance of civilized communities human beings survived as members of small hordes, in which the father ruled tyrannically over his sons and exercised absolute dominion over all women within the horde. The sons, in rebellion against the father's authority and from motives of sexual jealousy, united to murder the despotic patriarch and replaced the primal horde with a community in which they shared with each other equal status as brothers. The new brother band imposed such social and moral prohibitions as became necessary to suppress renewed violence toward figures identified with the absent patriarch, in René Girard's words, "to prevent people from being caught up in violent mimesis."[84] Feelings of liberation inevitably yielded to remorse for the crime and the community of sons soon mourned the loss of the father. Out of guilt for the criminal deed they undertook ritual acts of remembrance and atonement.

The totem feast—"perhaps mankind's earliest festival"[85]—originated as an act of collective memory and penance. The slaying and devouring of the sacrificial animal reproduced the murderous actions which the sons took against the primal father and revived the ambivalent emotions which surrounded the historical event. Members of the community demonstrated their reverence toward the totem animal—the father surrogate—and lamented its sacrifice, even as the ritual ceremony allowed them to celebrate the unity and liberation which followed the original deed. Thus the enactment of the feast transmitted the core of a dramatized identity: as equal participants in the banquet both celebrants and audience unconsciously identified themselves as the actors in the original scene of parricide. Through ritual simulation they projected the emotions of the primal horde onto the scene of the feast, while simultaneously distancing themselves from the criminal deed.

In the ancient world dramatization preserved contact with portions of the primal deed, but transformed that contact into stage actions, thereby placing greater distance between the scene and the audience, and between the actors and absent figures. Two modes of pagan dramaturgy succeeded totemistic reenactments: ceremonial sacrifice to the gods and the performance of tragedy within the amphitheater. Like William Robertson Smith, Freud concluded that ancient sacrificial rites had evolved directly from the ceremony of the totem feast. Within such Oedipal rites the absent figure of the father appeared not only as the sacrificial victim but as the god who received the devotional offering. The dual configuration represented both the ambivalent emotions associated with the primal deed and two distinct historical layers, "two chronologically successive meanings of the scene."[86] The father who fell to patricidal violence reappeared to the guilty sons as an idealized figure, a deity deserving of reverence. Freud, however, discovered the figure of Oedipus not only within sacrificial performances but also within the ancient amphitheater. On the classical stage the primal father returned not in the figure of the god but in the character of the hero whose sufferings drew the lamentations of the Chorus. The Greek tragic hero emerged from the Chorus—the community of brothers—as the single actor who accepted the guilt of the sons and therefore also the punishment which necessarily followed from it. He alone identified with the primal father as a figure of unavoidable and irredeemable suffering. His own fate embodied the primordial patriarch's destiny and the irrevocability of the original crime.

For Freud, as for Warburg, expressive movement within images originated in ceremonial reenactments of primal suffering. The phenomenon of mimesis thus represented the survival and transformation of an early ritual component within all creative artworks. In Freud's own view, mimesis ultimately derived from specific efforts at dramatizing the primal scene.

CHAPTER 3

Those stage creations and visual images which ranked among the most sublime accomplishments of civilization unconsciously revived a distant identity with the acts of primordial rebellion and mourning. At the totem feast and in the ancient amphitheater, dramatization thus revealed itself as an unceasing effort to restore the presence of an absent object.

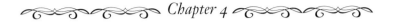 *Chapter 4*

Rhythms of Renewal:
Ernst Kris and Fritz Saxl

I

Freud's analysis of image-making and expressive movement in the visual arts culminated in his study of Gradiva and in the Renaissance essays written before the First World War. After 1914, however, the visual arts ceased to be a recurring interest in Freud's writing. While a concern with image-making and the creative process reappeared occasionally in his later work, painting and sculpture seemed to recede from view. In Vienna during the 1930s Ernst Kris, an art historian by education and profession, revived the ties between psychoanalysis and the study of visual art. As a student at the University of Vienna in the years immediately following the First World War, Kris received instruction from Emanuel Loewy and thus became acquainted early on with the effort to join the history of ancient art to the discipline of psychology, especially the study of memory. E. H. Gombrich, who, like Kris, attended Loewy's lectures as a student at the University of Vienna recalled the chief themes of Loewy's classes: "In his lectures and naturally in his exercises as well he frequently dealt with his theories of the rendering of nature in art, the migration of types, and later also theories of apotropaic symbolism."[1] Although he did not advocate a psychological approach to explaining artwork, Kris's doctoral advisor, Julius von Schlosser also emphasized in the history of art the manipulation and transmission of typical images.[2] Thus, even before his focus shifted to the psychology of art, Kris's training as an art historian introduced him to the problems of interpreting memory processes and tracking the survival of types.

As Kris preserved Freud's legacy in the psychology of visual art, so Fritz Saxl served as the inheritor and guardian of Aby Warburg's achievements. In that regard Saxl of course played an unrivaled role: he served for many years as Warburg's only assistant, and finally became Warburg's chosen successor to the directorship of the Library of Cultural Science in Hamburg.[3] As with the case of Kris, Saxl's family belonged to the Jewish professional middle class of Vienna; both art historians' fathers became successful lawyers.[4] Like Kris, Saxl departed from his father's career path, graduating from the University of Vienna in 1912 with a doctorate in art history. At the university Saxl studied with art historian Max Dvořák, who, as stated in the title of Dvořák's collection of essays, looked upon art history as the history of ideas. According to Dvořák, transformations in art were "always, initially, prompted by spiritual or intellectual developments."[5] Individual artworks reflected the characteristic ideas, or dominant spiritual tendencies, of their eras. Showing perhaps the influence of his early teacher, Saxl in his own later writings continued to seek in the visual arts indications of the "mental climate"[6] of past centuries.

During his university years Saxl spent long periods of time away from Vienna on his own travels and researches, including a stay in 1911 at the University of Berlin where he followed the lectures of Heinrich Wölfflin.[7] "Thousands of students," Saxl wrote years later, "heard him preach his gospel that the history of art is the history of artistic vision."[8] From Wölfflin's teachings Saxl preserved a respect for what he himself described as "historical aesthetic sensibility,"[9] or the capacity to comprehend the formal qualities and "visual subtleties"[10] of evolving artistic styles. Inspired by what Wölfflin called "descriptive art history,"[11] the traveling student sought a new language of art interpretation, a language which he found not in the Berlin lectures but in a secluded Hamburg library. To that isolated collection he brought an interest in finding the spirit in artworks and in explicating their visual nuances and mysteries.

In their backgrounds and early careers Kris and Saxl showed distinct similarities: a training which gave close attention to the formal qualities of artwork as indicators of psychological and visual types; an effort at reconceiving art history from the vantage point of an outside discipline; and guardianship of new movements in the interpretation of art. Further, Kris participated in projects organized by Saxl as director of the War-burg Library. Perhaps most significantly, a clear link between the two emerged in their own languages of art history. To explain the artist's cre-ative process Kris—the psychoanalyst—applied the concept "regression in the service of the ego."[12] Describing the metamorphosis of the visual arts from ancient to modern times Saxl—the cultural historian—employed the phrase: "regressive evolution."[13] As indicated in their terminologies, both the psychologist and the art historian interpreted individual creativity and historical change within art as processes of return and renewal. Regenera-tion of the past meant the manufacture of a new synthesis between ancient images and modern ideas. By reviving and reapplying ancient formulas, artists produced new modes of social communication and new frameworks within which to conceive contemporary needs. Ernst Kris explored artistic synthesis as a reflection of the ego's task of both mastering primal anxieties and emotions and expanding its engagement with current life and society. Fritz Saxl investigated that synthesis with the aim, in Carlo Ginzburg's words, "to free himself from the toils of a purely formalistic 'reading,' and to consider the individual work of art as a complex and active reac-tion (obviously *sui generis*) to the events of contemporary history."[14] Both researchers recognized patterns—or alternating intensities—to the resur-rection of primal images, and thus patterns also to the success with which artists confronted and enlivened those images. They perceived rhythms of renewal—both within the career of a single artist and within the sphere of culture at large.

II

Born in 1900, Ernst Kris entered the University of Vienna in the autumn of 1918, as the First World War came to its end. Having already visited the lectures of Dvořák and von Schlosser while a *Gymnasium* student, Kris adopted the formal study of art history, graduating in 1922 with his doctorate. Soon after graduation Kris attained the position of curator in the collection for sculpture and applied art at Vienna's *Kunsthistorisches Museum*. In 1924 Kris's fiancée, Marianne Rie, a medical student at the University of Vienna and the daughter of Sigmund Freud's physician, Oskar Rie, recommended the young art historian to the founder of psychoanalysis as an expert on cameos and intaglios, of which Freud possessed his own collection. Ernst Kris and Marianne Rie married in 1927. Both had determined to become psychoanalysts, and had completed their analytic training—Kris in Vienna and Rie in Berlin. In 1928 they joined the Vienna Psychoanalytic Society. For the next several years Kris contemplated exchanging his profession as an art historian for medical training and a career as a full-time psychoanalyst. In 1930 he became a lay teaching analyst at the Vienna Psychoanalytic Institute, but Freud encouraged him to keep his position at the *Kunsthistorisches Museum* as well. Two years later Freud named Kris as one of the new editors of *Imago*, where the art scholar soon published his first psychoanalytic studies of creativity. Until 1938, the year of the *Anschluss* and his forced emigration from Austria, Kris continued his work as both an art historian with the museum and a leading analyst within Freud's Viennese circle.[15]

Early in the 1930s Kris's work on the history and psychology of art brought him into contact with Saxl and the Warburg Library, a necessarily distant connection first with Hamburg and then London, but one which developed throughout the decade into a mutually beneficial relationship for Kris and the library. At the beginning of the decade Kris contributed to the compilation of the library's *Bibliography of the Survival of the Classics*, and invited his younger associate at the museum, Otto Kurz, to join the project. Importantly, the ties between the Viennese psychoanalyst and the Warburg Library extended beyond professional collaborations to include fundamental intellectual motives and concerns. In the years before the outbreak of the Second World War Kris's writings focused on issues which also drew concentrated attention from Warburgian scholars: the transmission of typical images or formulas in art history, and the cultural transition from ritual behavior and magical practices to artistic activities. Like Warburg, Kris concluded that the illusions of living movement and natural likeness within the visual arts derived in significant part from the survival of ancient types and the persistence of ritual influences. Still, while demonstrating an affinity for Warburgian studies and contributing to the library's endeavors, Kris explored ancient types and creative processes from a distinctly Viennese, Freudian perspective. Thus he investigated the preservation of antique formulas not only in typical visual images but also in the artist's imago—in the psychological model of creative genius which survived in legend and which internalized itself within the individual. The Viennese and Freudian perspectives again asserted themselves in his decision to elucidate principles of expression by exploring caricature and the art of communication through comic—even grimacing—masks.

Kris's first book on art and psychology, *Legend, Myth, and Magic in the Image of the Artist: A Historical Experiment* derived from early experiences as a student, curator, and psychoanalyst: the editorial assistance which he had contributed to Julius von Schlosser's compendium of writings about art and the artist from the Renaissance to the Enlightenment; his researches into the persistence of ancient formulas and pagan magical beliefs in Renaissance artwork; and his acquaintance with Viennese psychoanalytic interpretations of hero myths. Otto Kurz, who also had studied under von Schlosser at the University of Vienna, not only served as Kris's assistant at the *Kunsthistorisches Museum* but also became his collaborator on the project.[16] The book traced three formulaic images of the artist—hero, magic worker, and creative genius—through their ancient and Renaissance incarnations. The roots of each type reached beneath esoteric philosophies of art into legendary episodes and biographical anecdotes repeated of artists from generation to generation. Kris explained of his methodology that "the only significant factor is that an anecdote recurs, that it is recounted so frequently as to warrant the conclusion that it represents a typical image of the artist."[17] That approach led him beyond classical antiquity into the primal past, as "the anecdote in its wider sense taps the realms of myth and saga, from which it carries a wealth of imaginative material into recorded history."[18]

The heroic image of the artist emerged in the late classical period, attaching itself to Lysippus, the Greek sculptor from the age of Alexander credited by tradition with inspiring the imitation of nature in art. The chief elements of the heroic formula appeared in an anecdote recorded by Lysippus' near contemporary Duris of Samos and retold by Pliny the Elder in his *Natural History*. By trade a coppersmith, Lysippus supposedly turned to painting upon hearing by chance the comment of the painter Eupompus, who stated that in his own pictures he followed not the examples of predecessors but only those of nature itself. Transforming himself into an artist, the uninstructed Lysippus subsequently initiated a naturalist revolution in art for which he achieved widespread fame. The outstanding features of that ancient story—that Lysippus required no teacher, that fortune alone inspired his radical professional decision, that he rose from lowly stature to exalted social status, and that only nature provided him with models—reappeared during the Renaissance in legends of the life of Giotto. In Vasari's rendering, the young Giotto, while acting as a shepherd to his peasant father's flock, made drawings of the animals in his care. By a fortunate accident, Cimabue came across Giotto at work, perceived his skill, and ensured that he received training. Giotto conformed to the ancient heroic model: a commoner, born with artistic talent and impelled from youth to express his prodigal talent by copying nature, received the chance opportunity from a master artist to elevate both his skill and his rank within society.

The painter's imago thus held roots in traditional hero myths, according to which the heroic figure, abandoned in childhood by exalted parents, lived as an outcast until fate revealed his noble or divine origins and prepared him to become a builder of empires and a defender of civilization. The typical anecdote of the artist's youth conformed to that primordial model, emphasizing not only the artist's isolated early development but also his exalted genealogy—a lineage which Lysippus acquired by identifying himself with Eupompos, and which Giotto gained by accepting the patronage of Cimabue. The mythic sources of the formula of the heroic artist revealed its psychological motivations. In one of the earliest applications of psychoanalysis to cultural studies, Sigmund Freud and his Viennese disciple Otto Rank had traced the psychological meaning of hero myths to the "family romance," a common childhood fantasy in which the child pictured himself as the offspring not of his actual parents but of far more highly-placed ones, and thus also imagined for himself a predestined, heroic future.[19] The Renaissance image of the artist carried an emotional resonance identical to that which Freud and Rank attributed to the hero myth: "On the basis of this psychological foundation we can understand that the anecdote concerning Giotto's youth itself functioned like a motif of mythological thinking and thus was able to migrate far afield. One has the impression that it expresses an intensely satisfying idea of the youth of artists—an idea that for this reason was capable of wide diffusion."[20]

Biographies of the artist from antiquity to the Renaissance also distributed vivid accounts of the artist's incorruptible commitment, in particular his devotion to "art as *mimesis*, as the imitation of nature,"[21] and his acceptance of a divinely inspired vision. In consequence of his skill at copying nature, the artist appeared as a magician or illusionist. As a divinely motivated, creative spirit, he acquired the image of a genius.

In the classical and Renaissance worlds an intriguing and tenacious formula described the seemingly magical powers of the painter and sculptor: "The anecdote tells us that the artist's product is mistaken for reality, that the portrait is taken for what it portrays."[22] Such stories recirculated a formula traceable to the sixth-century myth of Daedelus, the artisan who sculpted automatons—figures capable of generating their own movement. Similar archaic traditions related how Hephaestus, the immortal craftsman, produced for the gods objects with the power of self-motion. The mythological belief in the artisan's supernatural gifts survived in later legends of the artist as an expert illusionist who manufactured within his artwork the appearance of organic movement: "Motion and life, which in mythology had a literal meaning, became pale metaphors, and the simile, 'So true to nature that the work of art creates the illusion of life and movement,' was retained in the legend."[23] The mythology of the artisan's miracle-working powers originated in primitive ritual magic and the belief in the identity between images and their original objects, a belief most clearly manifest in the production of effigies and in the attempt to control, influence, or supplicate objects through their substitutes. Aby Warburg, Kris noted, demonstrated the persistence of effigy belief as a motive in the creation of Renaissance statues.[24] The identification of image and object revealed itself further in legends of image-makers who sought through painting or sculpture to restore the life, or preserve the memory, of deceased loved ones. The conviction in an identity between images and what they depicted possessed deep emotional force—and "continues to live on in the unconscious of men."[25]

In ritual practices the magic of an image, or the belief in its identity with its object, did not depend upon any visual resemblance between the picture and what it portrayed. In the history of image-making the quest for likeness in fact emerged only with the decline of magical belief: "At the dawn of Greek art, when the belief in the identity of picture and depicted was prevalent, there was little or no concern with making the work of art as lifelike as possible; in subsequent eras when this belief was on the wane, naturalism was regarded as a distinct accomplishment of the artist."[26] Thus, only with the late classical period did stories praise the artist for his ability to manufacture the illusion of reality. Such adulatory anecdotes, in which an "artist's handiwork closes the gap separating picture and depicted,"[27] preserved in the new language of naturalism the still underlying, primordial conviction in the magical identity between an image and its object. In the following centuries, Christian writers of late antiquity and the Middle Ages detected within the lifelike composition of classical sculpture not the decline of magic but the ancient signs of image worship. The Renaissance found in the realism of ancient art a new source of inspiration but still looked fearfully upon the power of such living images. The visual arts evolved culturally from ritual practices and magical techniques not as a development in which art superseded ritual but as a series of stages which joined ritualist and naturalist elements in new combinations and intensities. From a psychological point of view, the image of the artist as illusionist reflected an effort at internal synthesis— between the conviction that an artist created likeness and the primal belief that an artist created life.

Divine inspiration, which the classical period had attributed first to poets, figured prominently in the Hellenistic notion of the painter or sculptor as a magician. Divine inspiration led the artist beyond manufacturing lifelike copies to creating examples of beauty and a sense of life not found in nature. In ancient and Renaissance anecdotes the artist observed and remembered details from the external world but in the process of creation painted or sculpted figures according to his own inward models. One typical story described artists who reproduced complete figures after observing only a single detail of their originals, and who thus demonstrated "the possession of that 'internal figure' which, in Dürer's words, is the mark of the *divino artista*."[28] To create from one's own vision, whether from divine inspiration or inward compulsion, became the sign of artistic genius, a formula which gained new force during the Renaissance and which persisted into the nineteenth century when it "culminated in the tendency to view the work of art more and more as an expression of the artist's 'soul.'"[29] Thus did the unconscious, mythic belief in divinely inspired talent survive in synthesis with the modern formula of the artist as a self-conscious creator moved by a unique vision. The strength of that psychological synthesis revealed itself in still another guise in efforts by critics and psychiatrists to interpret an artwork as symptomatic of the creator's personality: both literary biography and medical pathographies "insist on seeing the artist's life and work as one and the same thing."[30] Critical of such reductionist approaches, Kris did not exempt his own notion of the artist from scrutiny. The formula of the divine artist emphasized—as did his own researches—"the crucial importance of creative activity to his inner life."[31] In the final passages of the book Kris speculated on the influence which recurring formulas exerted not only on the work of cultural scientists, but also on the artist's own career: artists themselves unconsciously accepted the fate delineated by ancient anecdotes through what Kris called "enacted biography."[32]

Kris and Kurz focused their book chiefly on a Warburgian theme: the transmission of typical formulas and the preservation of pagan beliefs within such types. In 1934—the same year in which the book appeared—Kris presented to the Vienna Psychoanalytic Society a paper which expanded upon his own concept of enacted biography.[33] Biographical formulas established models which survived not only in mythological and literary traditions, but also through their "enactment."[34] The internalization and acting out of such models described a primordial process: "In a world whose semi-darkness is again and again submerged in myths, the boundary between the individual and tradition grows hazy and identification with the ancestor decides the nature and direction of the individual's existence."[35] Examples of the primal process of identification surfaced in contemporary society among those who "live even today the life of a biographical type, the 'destiny' of a particular class, rank, or profession."[36] More generally, the incorporation of elements of biographical formulas figured noticeably in personality development, especially during adolescence and in the final consolidation of the super-ego.

In tracing the artist's imago from its appearance in legend to its role in biography, Kris—like Warburg and Freud before him—followed a route from the study of image-making to the investigation of enactments. Painters and sculptors did not merely create external likeness but instilled such likeness with a sense of mimetic vitality or organic self-motion: "the work of art is admired for its power to convey life—we may say, for the sake of its magic aliveness."[37] Mimetic impulses strove not simply toward resemblance but toward the simulation and regeneration of an absent object. Just as the creative artist brought life to images in his work, so too he reenacted the ancient formulas in his own biography. Thus did Kris begin to conceive of creativity in both art and experience as a rhythm of renewal, or as he described it in his studies of caricature and the comic, a regression which served the ego.

III

In the years before the Second World War, Kris studied not sublime likenesses in art but the exaggerations and distortions of likeness found in caricature—both the intentional caricatures of cartoons and portraiture and the unintentional ones of psychotic creations. Such creations revealed the process of the ego's regression and its attempts—successful and unsuccessful—at self-renewal. Whereas Kris traced biographical formulas to the recounting of mythological anecdotes, he linked the art of caricature, which preserved formulas of physical expression, to the donning of masks. Like anecdotes, masks produced uniquely vivid impressions while simultaneously adhering to preordained formulas. Indeed, masks epitomized the ambiguities of the creative process. Simultaneously defensive and expressive, self-protective and demonstrative, the mask embodied an ancient type in the sense not of a rigid abstraction but of an uneasy synthesis of regressive and regenerative motives, a synthesis from which art derived originating impulses. Within the context of stage enactments, masks separated the audience from accustomed visual reality so as to convey to them the presence of creatively restored objects. To transform masks into instruments with which actors communicated to spectators and at the same time preserved the audience's distance from the stage action marked an achievement of ancient drama. With his exploration of caricature, Kris entered the world of the amphitheater.[38]

In a paper presented to the Vienna Psychoanalytic Society in 1932, and published the following year in *Imago*, Kris examined masked and caricatured expressions by focusing on the work of Franz Xaver Messerschmidt (1736–1783), German artist and professor of sculpture at the Academy in Vienna. Borrowing essential features from the typical image of the artist, Messerschmidt's biography included accounts of his working as a shepherd, his developing early talent by carving figures of animals, and his displaying magical powers. Reliable contemporary records of his life, however, indicated the onset of severe psychic illness, dating perhaps to his first apprenticeship and becoming irreversible during his appointment at the Academy. The illness, which Kris described as "a psychosis with predominating paranoid trends,"[39] reached the point at which Messerschmidt believed himself possessed by demons with whom he engaged in a constant struggle for control. Throughout his illness and in his final years of isolation, Messerschmidt continued to produce sculpture, concentrating his efforts almost exclusively on molding a series of busts, or character heads, all of which displayed severely distended or agitated features (Figure 17). In those extraordinarily distorted or caricatured expressions Kris perceived the sculptor's attempt at psychological synthesis and self-restoration.

Grimacing surfaced repeatedly in Messerschmidt's sculpted figures. As Kris explained, the grimace appeared in human visage either as an intent to convey aggression or as "a miscarried expressive movement"[40]—a piece of failed expression in which aggressive drives disrupted or overwhelmed the ego's self-control and ability to communicate. The dual nature of grimacing evidenced the divided origin of all human expressive movement— as movement which establishes contact and conveys a message and which at the same time " 'does not speak to us' "[41] but harbors instead an inward, private meaning that places a barrier between the self and others. The

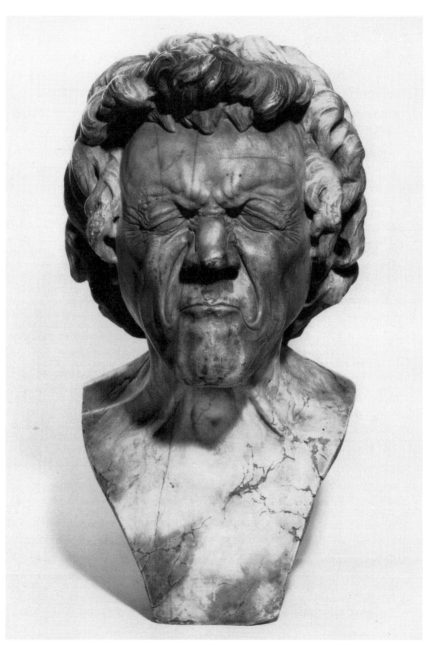

17. Franz Xaver Messerschmidt, Character head, *Ein abgezehrter Alter mit Augenschmerzen* (a haggard old man with painful eyes). Vienna, Österreichische Galerie Belvedere. Photo: Fotostudio Otto/Österreichische Galerie Belvedere, Vienna.

facial expressions on Messerschmidt's busts possessed a predominantly and necessarily private significance: grimaces gave him power over the demons that tortured him. The sculptor repeatedly scrutinized in mirrors his own grimacing expressions and preserved in marble the "mimic constellations"[42] of his face which provided him with a sense of protection. Similar in their motivation to archaic defensive images as Loewy described them, Messerschmidt's sculptures represented a private effort at "warding off, or intimidating, the demons."[43] Indeed, such artwork reflected "a regression to magical behavior," specifically a resort to the "apotropaic or defensive magic" found in primitive rituals, a prominent feature of which had been the "use of masks."[44] Messerschmidt's sculpture thus recalled the origin of masks in the defensive aim of the grimace and revived their primal function as agents of self-protection and counteraggression.

Yet, the artist's case also demonstrated how the ego sought through the creation of masks—or of mimic constellations—to restore its sense of self-control and self-direction and to open a path of communication with others. Several among the numerous busts which the sculptor produced in his years of illness indicated that Messerschmidt endeavored to give natural proportion and subtlety of expression to his troubled works. Still, the uniformly strained features and stereotyped grimace reappeared and dominated the surface. As Kris wrote, "we can hardly escape the notion that we are here dealing with a person who struggles before the mirror for a genuine facial expression in order to retain the rapidly vanishing contact with the environment. It is an attempt in which he fails."[45] Messerschmidt's art demonstrated "an attempt at restitution"[46]—an effort on the part of the ego to revive its autonomy, self-mastery, and engagement with the world. In that defeated effort "the readily comprehensible facial expression is replaced by a system of rigid mimic constellations."[47] The stylized, unnatural masks carved by Messerschmidt proved unusable for social contact and interaction. Severe illness prevented the sculptor from synthesizing the personal meanings of his masks with the goal of communicating to an audience at a distance from himself: "In the ideal case these meanings cannot be separated from the whole of the structure; presumably all details and traits are socially meaningful."[48] The inward, regressive forces which inspired Messerschmidt's production perpetually undermined his efforts at artistically and psychologically reintegrating those forces. The sculptor's masks functioned as servants of a private, ritual performance rather than as instruments of a dramatic enactment.[49]

If Messerschmidt's work represented a failed attempt at dramaturgic contact with the world, the intentional distortions of caricature successfully engaged the minds and emotions of audiences, despite the presence of elements which continually endangered such contact. Belief in the identity between an image and its object—essential to ritual magic—persisted within the art of caricature, for which "distortion of the image here, too, 'represents' a distortion of its original."[50] Through that distortion the caricaturist performed an act of aggression against the object, an act, however, which threatened to alienate his audience. To engage the imagination of his public he therefore included within his exaggerated portraits such features of resemblance as served to generate pleasure from comic comparison and recognition. Meaningful caricature thus demanded a difficult synthesis of ancient effigy belief and modern devotion to naturalism. Magical aggressive purposes and comedic enjoyment of likeness had to reinforce, not combat, each other: "The comic effect produced by a comparison and the effect of an ingeniously concealed tendency react one upon the other."[51] Aggressive drives motivated effective caricatures; the creation of likeness preserved their contact with the audience, preventing them from degenerating into private, illusionist acts. Thus did the caricaturist provide a model of "regression in the service of the ego:"[52] hostile, magical drives and play with resemblances combined with each other to produce a critical and communicative art.

In 1933—the year in which Kris's essay on Messerschmidt and psychotic art appeared—Austrian chancellor Engelbert Dollfuss dissolved the Parliament in Vienna. In the next year—during which Kris published his work on legends of the artist and on caricature—Dollfuss violently suppressed the Austrian Social Democratic party and labor movement and established a Catholic, authoritarian regime under his *Vaterländische Front*. As Gombrich recalled, the political chill spread to the museum: "Kris was deeply aware of all the undercurrents of resistance he had to encounter within the Museum and in the University. Unlike many who were in the same situation he did not close his eyes to these dangers. On the contrary, he kept them wide open. He made a point of reading the *Völkische Beobachter* and he had no illusions. In Austria itself the scene had also darkened with the abolition of Parliament and the establishment of a dictatorship. It was when telling an anti-government joke at the office and being met with frozen stares that Kris began to reflect on the instability of the effect of the comic. The invitation to share in a mild form of aggression had led to embarrassment all round."[53] In response to the Dollfuss coup, Kris sought a secure position for his colleague, Otto Kurz, and in 1933 recommended the Jewish art historian to Fritz Saxl. As a result, Kurz, who had been beaten by anti-Semitic youths while a student at the University of Vienna, received a grant to work with Saxl at the library in Hamburg. When the institution moved at the end of 1933 to London, Kurz rejoined it, and in the following year a member of the Warburg family provided him with a grant to assist Kris in researching the topic of effigy magic and the prohibition against image-making.[54] In 1934, he and Kris dedicated their study of legends of the artist to the Warburg Library of Cultural Science.[55]

In opposition to conditions in authoritarian Austria, which sharply narrowed the ego's scope of action and art's critical freedom, Kris sought to revive and exhibit earlier products of caricaturists. Suggesting to his new assistant, Gombrich, that they collaborate to write a history of caricature, Kris began the project in 1934 and continued it through 1935, until he secured an assistantship for Gombrich with Saxl at the Warburg Library in London.[56] As Gombrich explained, during their collaboration Kris "arranged a Daumier Exhibition in Vienna to help us with our researches, but also to have the pleasure of displaying subversive cartoons and to collaborate with French colleagues."[57] In the spring of 1937 Kris traveled briefly to London where he presented the results of his and Gombrich's joint research to the Warburg Library. The paper completed Kris's work on caricature but at the same time explicitly demonstrated the possibilities of joining Warburgian and Freudian approaches to the study of art.

In caricature, Kris explained at the library, the subject's portrait "is boiled down to an easily remembered formula."[58] That formula appeared most frequently as a simplified sketch with qualities resembling the unconscious techniques found in dreams, jokes, and children's play: the distortion or condensation of identifying characteristics, the representation of the whole by a part, the use of visual allusion and analogy. The creation and transmission of a formulaic sketch revealed the controlled application of primary psychological mechanisms, in the case of caricature, "a process where—under the influence of aggression—primitive structures are used to ridicule the victim."[59] The freedom to pursue caricature—to employ primary mechanisms in portrait art—accompanied the shift in the image of the artist which occurred toward the end of the sixteenth century, when modern caricature drawings first appeared and gained acceptance. At that time—at the peak of the Renaissance—the image of the artist as one who copied nature yielded to the model of the inspired creator who produced from an inward picture. Audiences seeking the creator's vision conferred unique value on the sketch "as the most direct document of inspiration."[60] Among painters and sculptors themselves the transformed image of the artist helped to introduce a new era of "play with form."[61] Thus artistic and historical conditions at the end of the Renaissance supported a new type of playful experimentation, or "controlled regression,"[62] in the visual arts: portrait caricature.

Comparing the force of visual imagery to that of language in the development of the individual and of culture, Kris concluded: "The visual image has deeper roots, is more primitive."[63] Belief in the magical power of images therefore possessed a primal energy which the caricaturist mobilized in his drawings: "Under the surface of fun and play the old image magic is still at work."[64] The caricaturist, however, reasserted his mastery over magical thinking. Transforming a likeness did not imply a magical action against the original but instead "presupposes a degree of security, at distance from action."[65] During the creative process, the ego thus initially relinquished mastery over primary forms of thought and communication so as to participate in the primordial activity of image magic. The reclaiming of mastery required that the artist reestablish psychological distance from primal magic, a process of recovery which recalled Warburg's concept of reflective space and his conception of art as a spiritualized taking of distance. According to Kris, however, the mechanism of distancing belonged to the process of controlled regression, a process which allowed the successful artist, and the successfully operating ego, to utilize primary

psychological mechanisms of image-making and play acting while return-
ing to full and dynamic engagement with the world of the present.

That attempted synthesis of psychological functioning Kris also explored in his 1936 essay on the artwork of psychotically ill patients. Psychotic painting and drawing reflected the ego's effort at restitution—at
reestablishing or strengthening contact with the world—through art. Levels of success at restitution revealed themselves in stylistic tendencies, as in
the case of the Swedish artist Ernst Josephson, who as an adult descended
into a psychotic, delusional state. Prior to the appearance of illness, Josephson devoted himself to realist painting, thereby "attempting to resist the
onslaught of regression."[66] After the emergence of severe illness, however,
he restricted himself chiefly to "contour drawings"[67] characterized by two
outstanding features. In the first place "we find a fusion and combination
of various divergent elements which are of a distinctly symbolic nature, but
the logic of their fusion escapes our comprehension."[68] Second, "the representation of the human figure is particularly rigid and stiff, impressing
us as unnatural and artificial."[69] Those characteristics appeared not only
in the drawings of a master burdened with mental illness but also in the
creations of unskilled psychotic patients.

The "fusion of forms"[70] which typified psychotic creations originated
in the primary process. Images which joined human figures to natural
objects, which combined several heads or faces in one whole, or which
created a single visage from the features of different persons manifested
the process of condensation and symbol formation which occurred within
the unconscious. In jokes a similar fusion emerged in wordplay. In the
case of artistic efforts it appeared instead as "play on shapes,"[71] a process
evident in caricature, as well as in psychotic products. Indeed, that fusion,
or aesthetic play, helped to explain the essential ambiguity of visual depictions: "Configurations which bear the imprint of the primary process tend
to be ambiguous, allowing for more than one interpretation."[72] With the
irony inherent to his art the portrait caricaturist used the fusion of forms
simultaneously to shape a likeness and to "unmask"[73] his object, and so
brought the ambiguity of playful imagery into the service of criticism. By
contrast, the creative combinations and products of the psychotic patient

did not reflect artistic synthesis but instead remained dominated by the primary process, which merely "unifies their facade."[74] Behind that facade, the elements of psychotic creations retained their magical intentions.

Psychotic portraits produced imaginative combinations but scant human expression. To the contrary, facial expressions presented a blank surface, a fixed or empty appearance: as a rule "they do not supply a clue to the moods or the personality or its characteristics and thus do not invite identification."[75] The impossibility of producing an identity with others reflected the psychotic artist's deeper loss of mimic functioning and communication. "Human mimic expression," Kris explained, "is addressed to the other person; it aims at contact. It is this contact which, during the schizophrenic process, is loosened and in catatonic conditions, broken."[76] In portraits of himself or others the psychotic patient depicted human expressions as the projections of his own troubled motions or gestures. The creative artist too had to remain aware of the same hazard of projection: Leonardo, Kris recalled, warned the painter against "the tendency to substitute his own bodily experience for that of the model he wants to depict."[77] Psychotics could not detach their portrait art from "the disturbance of their own expressive movements."[78] Thus their mimetic creations— their artistic likenesses—rigidified into frozen masks.

The attempt at restitution revealed itself as a desperate dramaturgic effort. Artist-patients sought to renew expressive contact with the world through the production of masks but could not free those masks from archaic immobility and magical expectation. Their creations degenerated into magically fixed gestures and expressions offering no opportunity for restored communication or mental autonomy. Their products tended always to draw the audience away from observing the artwork and toward participating in its mysterious purpose. In both patients and artists, restitution aimed not only at revived contact and communication but at restoring absent figures: "the mechanism of projection in artistic creation," Kris stated, "also serves the reparation of introjected, and hence lost, objects."[79] The spirit of the Greek stage thus infused successful artistic projection, through which "the object emerges anew, with full—at times even enhanced—reality for the artist and the community whom he addresses."[80] Restitution required a dramatic achievement: the ego of the artist patient sought its uncertain recovery by employing the dramaturgy of the ancient amphitheater.

IV

As demonstrated by attempts at inward restitution, art reflected an effort at self-renewal and revived engagement with the world, a psychological process which Kris reexamined closely in the final years before the outbreak of the Second World War. During his visit to London in 1937, the Viennese psychoanalyst not only delivered a presentation at the Warburg Library but gave a paper before the British Psycho-Analytical Society, discussing how comic processes illuminated aspects of ego development. The comic effect of words, gestures, or visual images originated in the enjoyment of play, through which children gained command over language, movements, and objects. Wordplay or comic action produced a sense of enjoyment from comparing in oneself moments of unsuccessful and successful command, or from comparing the divergent levels of command between oneself and the comic figure. Through comedy the ego reexperienced not only the achievement of mastery but also "the pleasure arising from a sense of mastery."[81] Such pleasure derived from triumphing over a fear. Thus comic enjoyment revived the satisfaction which the ego first experienced through playful experimentation and repetition following the perception of a danger: "Comic pleasure, according to this hypothesis, refers to a past achievement of the ego which has required long practice to bring it about."[82] The comic repeated a rhythm of play which began with a sensation of anxiety and ended with a feeling of renewal. In Kris's words: "Repetition means a return and a rediscovery."[83] On rare occasions the comic process or sensibility enabled the ego to achieve "a permanent transformation;" far more often, however, "the victory of the ego is transitory."[84] The rhythm of renewal thus resumed its course.

That same rhythm appeared as part of the creative process in literary as well as visual arts, as Kris indicated in a paper which he delivered to the London Institute of Psycho-Analysis in 1938 and which he expanded for publication after the war. Through literature the ego transformed a playful reenactment or daydream designed to master a traumatic conflict into a narrative capable of engaging an audience. The invention of effective narrative demonstrated the ego's growing sense of command and its successful detachment from the original trauma: it evidenced "the increasing distance from direct reaction to the traumatic experience, distance from immediacy of discharge."[85] That distance protected the psychological sphere in which the ego performed the task of renewal, a process which Kris described vividly for the visual arts and which deserves to be quoted here in full:

> The artist does not "render" nature, nor does he "imitate" it, but he creates it anew. He controls the world through his work. In looking at the object that he wishes to "make," he takes it in with his eyes until he feels himself in full possession of it. Drawing, painting, and carving what has been incorporated and is made to reemerge from vision, is a two-pronged activity. Every line or every stroke of the chisel is a simplification, a reduction of reality. The unconscious meaning of this process is control at the price of destruction. But destruction of the real is fused with construction of its image: When lines merge into shapes, when the new configuration arises, no "simile" of nature is given. Independent of the level of resemblance, nature has been re-created."[86]

Artistic production proceeded from a rhythm of restitution according to which the ego reduced the world to its elements so as to rebuild its image and to regain a sense of autonomous control. That process occurred also within the audience, who in the course of observing an artwork passed inwardly from the phase of identifying with the psychological model portrayed in the artist's product to "the stage in which we 'imitate' the strokes and lines with which it was produced."[87] Ultimately, spectators too participated in the rhythm of the ego's renewal: "we end as co-creators."[88] As Arnold Hauser argued, psychoanalysis made its essential contribution to art history by teaching "that the artist's way to his work leads through a loss of reality, and that his way back to reality is a result of his work."[89] The artist's production and the audience's cooperation derived from that rhythm of absence and return.

The *Anschluss* between Nazi Germany and Austria caused the irreparable rupture—the break in the opportunity of renewal—in Kris's life in Vienna. In his immediate world of the art museum the direction of events had become increasingly clear since the Dollfuss coup. In 1936, for example, Hans Sedlmayr had succeeded to Julius von Schlosser's chair in art history at the university. Sedlmayr had been a member of the Nazi party in 1932–1933 and openly welcomed the *Anschluss.*[90]

In 1938 Kris permanently left Vienna for London, where Freud too found refuge, and in the following year, began working as a researcher and advisor to the British Broadcasting Corporation, helping to coordinate interpretation of Nazi radio propaganda. In 1940, less than a year after Freud's death, Kris accepted the assignment of establishing an office for propaganda analysis in Canada, soon performing the same duty in New York, where he emigrated in September 1940. Kris received a visiting professorship at the New School for Social Research, and in 1941, with German émigré sociologist Hans Speier, initiated at the school a program to investigate Nazi home broadcasts, the results of which the two published in 1944 under the title *German Radio Propaganda.* Supported by the Rockefeller Foundation's Research Project on Totalitarian Communication, Kris and Speier coordinated their work with another member of the foundation's effort, émigré film historian Siegfried Kracauer, who undertook research at the Museum of Modern Art into German film propaganda. After the war, Kris helped to organize research into child development at the Yale Child Study Center, also directing a study of adolescence at the New York Psychoanalytic Institute. He died at an early age in 1957.[91]

In his studies of wartime propaganda Kris considered for virtually the last time the problem of the transmission of images, now from an aspect determined by immediate political events. "The German propagandist," Kris and Speier wrote, "talks about the world to his audience in terms of images."[92] Betraying "a compound of cynicism and mysticism,"[93] the propagandist pieced together images for which he claimed the authenticity of tradition: "The propagandist is convinced that his imagery has grown deep roots among the German people. He assumes that it has become so familiar that whenever he exposes only part of an image the public will tend to supply the rest. He hopes that this tendency will be an obstacle to reasonable examination of the meaning of his words and that the urge toward completing a familiar pattern will take the place of thinking."[94] German propaganda not only sought to manufacture formulaic images but intended those images to overwhelm the ego and its criticism. The world of that propaganda produced its "stage," "actors," and "situations" but aimed only at their fusion.[95] In that artificial performance world "the self is reduced to Hitler, the satraps under his command, the Party, and the German soldier."[96] The propagandist kept the chorus on stage, but deprived it of its own voice and comprehending vision: "The chorus repeats the tale. Neutrals praise Germany or blame the foe."[97] The dramatic sphere in which the self, actors, and audience found restitution—an autonomous reengagement with the world—collapsed entirely: "The propagandist stage manager creates a situation in which ritual becomes event, and in which individuals and groups are meant to lose their identity and be fused together into one acting whole."[98] Thus did the threat represented by German propaganda express itself as the destruction of the legacy of the amphitheater."

Like Freud after the First World War, Kris devoted himself after the Second World War to problems of ego development and adaptation. Like Freud, after the long period of wartime existence Kris turned away from studying the visual arts. His final essays on art, written in the years immediately following 1945, focused on creativity and interpretation in poetry rather than on painting and sculpture. Still, one such essay—examining the problem of poetic ambiguity—brought to culmination a line of thought which Kris had begun to pursue in his early studies of caricature and psychotic creations.

Kris's 1948 essay on the language of poetry opened with the following definition of art: "a process of communication and re-creation, in which ambiguity plays a central role."[99] Art manifested what Kris described as integrative ambiguity, through which "manifold meanings evoke and support one another."[100] Within poetry and the creative work of art, "though multiple, the meaning is unified."[101] Pictures or words which conveyed that integrated, aesthetic ambiguity originated in the overdetermined images or language of the primary psychic process. Not only did the artist resurrect those condensed unconscious meanings in his work but the audience again revived them in its response to the artwork and in the subsequent process of interpretation: "Communication," Kris wrote, "lies not so much in the prior intent of the artist as in the consequent re-creation by the audience of his work of art."[102] Artwork and poetry, however, only produced an aesthetic effect by generating "a shift in *psychic distance*," or what Kris also referred to here as "detachment."[103] Without the creation of distance, artworks became "transformed to pin-up and propaganda, magic and ritual."[104] Thus artistic form not only transmitted a unified complex of meanings but also indicated how elements of that complex were to be "responded to at shifting distances."[105] Successful art allowed the ego to control the distance between image and object, and therefore preserve self-autonomy.

The ability to encounter art at shifting distances described a psychological rhythm of regression and self-restitution. That rhythm had also belonged to the world of the ancient stage—a world of objects created anew, of masked enactments and communications which called on the spectator to recognize and tolerate ambiguities and to guard judgment against the magical belief in a real identity between image and object. In Kris's postwar statement on art the ancient spirit of the amphitheater rose against the modern spirit of the propaganda broadcast.

V

During his years as an itinerant student—still officially enrolled at the University of Vienna—Fritz Saxl encountered Aby Warburg. In 1911, having attended Wölfflin's lectures at the University of Berlin, Saxl continued on his journey through German archives and galleries, ultimately arriving in the art historical precincts of Hamburg. During his sojourn in the city, he decided to visit Warburg at his library, less from his interest in the history of art than from his own curiosity about the history of astrological symbols. Warburg painstakingly demonstrated to the young student that art and astrology belonged together within the wider study of image-making, impressing Saxl not only with his scholarly exposition but also with his sense of intellectual and personal conviction. Warburg had adopted the study of images as his own, and at their first meeting he quietly encouraged Saxl to do the same. In 1913, Saxl's two predecessors having departed the library, Warburg invited the recent Viennese graduate to serve as his new research assistant. Saxl accepted the offer and settled in Hamburg. During a visit to Florence in the spring of 1914 the two scholars first discussed broadening the library into a full research institution, a plan which collapsed only months later with the outbreak of war. The Austrian army assigned Saxl to an artillery observation post on the Austro-Italian frontier, where he remained for the duration of the conflict. From the Italian border he corresponded with Warburg, recounting in one letter that while on patrol he once heard Tuscan dialect spoken across the line: "Even in that moment it sounded like music."[106] Questions connected with the expansion of the library continued to occupy Saxl's mind. In the spring of 1918, while recovering from a wound, he began to map out his future research in the collection. With the end of the war, however, he returned to Vienna, his future once more a matter of uncertainty.[107]

In 1920, the Warburgs and the work of the library led Saxl again to make Hamburg his home. In response to a request from the family Saxl agreed to manage the Warburg Library as its acting director while Aby Warburg recovered from the mental illness which, having threatened him for years, had finally overtaken him. The traveling scholar and research assistant of prewar years resumed what now became a permanent career, guiding the library's transformation into an academic institute and forging links between it and the world of formal university scholarship. After Warburg's death in 1929, Saxl succeeded his mentor as the institute's official director, having already contributed significantly to the emergence of Hamburg as a new center of higher learning in Germany. The Nazi rise to power, however, forced upon him the existence once more of an itinerant scholar. In 1933 Warburg's brothers negotiated the library's safe removal from Hitler's Germany to London, where Saxl now sought to preserve and even extend the scholarly and professional activities of a research institution virtually unknown within its new home. With the outbreak of the Second World War, Saxl devoted himself to sustaining the library's work under difficult conditions on the home front, and, as an émigré scholar, to integrating that work with Britain's war effort. In 1945, with the Warburg Institute permanently established in London, he turned his energies toward defining its postwar, international identity. In 1948 Saxl died, only three years after the defeat of Nazi Germany.

For thirty-five years he had served as a tireless assistant and successor to Warburg, preserving, expanding, and publicizing Warburg's legacy during a prolonged period of political crisis, war, and exile.[108]

In a lecture delivered at Reading University in the year before his death, Saxl offered to a British audience a succinct explanation of the approach to art history which the Warburg school followed at that time, and which Saxl had consistently pursued in his own career. The humanities in general, and the study of art in particular, he stated, showed "that images with a meaning peculiar to their own time and place, once created, have a magnetic power to attract other ideas into their sphere; that they can suddenly be forgotten and remembered again after centuries of oblivion."[109] Saxl's statement—an art historical rendering of the return of the repressed—drew his listeners' attention not only to history but to psychology. Like Kris, he attributed a primary psychological force—a magnetic influence—to the visual image. The explanation he provided at Reading, however, indicated not only how Saxl perceived the role of psychology in art history but also how he understood and fulfilled his function as official representative of the Warburg school.

Since first joining the Warburg Library, Saxl had attempted to bring the institution into contact with wider scholarly and nonexpert, but interested audiences. In that persistent effort Saxl valued highly the contemporary phenomenon of the slide lecture, through which he brought the impact of old images directly before new publics. At the end of the First World War he had experimented with pictorial images as educational tools when he organized, under the aegis of the new Austrian Socialist government, a Viennese exhibition entitled "No More Wars," for which he included reprints of Goya's etchings, *The Disasters of War*.[110] In 1923 an early opportunity to organize a visual lecture for a nonspecialist audience presented itself when he assisted his mentor in selecting photographic slides to accompany Warburg's Kreuzlingen lecture on Pueblo ritual.[111] During the next twenty-five years, in Hamburg and in England, Saxl utilized the slide lecture format to combine the compact, reflective mode of the essay with the immediacy of visual demonstration, and thereby produce a direct appeal to differing groups of listeners. Writing his presentations in full before delivering them, Saxl did not subordinate word to image, but carefully adjusted the one to the other. His lectures, which spanned his years as director of the Warburg Library from the first postwar period to the second, reflected not only how he interpreted the essential discoveries of the Warburg school but also how his own thought evolved under the changing fortunes of his career and the pressures of his time.

VI

In Hamburg immediately following the First World War Saxl took personal responsibility not only to maintain Warburg's collection during his mentor's recovery at Kreuzlingen but also to expand the library according to the vision which the two had formulated in Florence. The founding of the University of Hamburg in 1920 created the conditions for that expansion. Upon his return from Switzerland in 1924, Warburg received an honorary professorship from the university, as would Saxl after him. In 1926, construction of Warburg's Library of Cultural Science marked the collection's new status within Hamburg academia and within the German scholarly world at large. Warburg's death and the onset of the depression brought that first period of rapid institutional development to a close. The spread of anti-Semitism within the universities and the growth of the Nazi movement foreshadowed the library's ultimate fate in Germany.

In 1925—at the height of the library's expansion, with Warburg recovered and once more at work, and with the new research building under construction—Saxl presented at Hamburg's *Kunsthalle* a lecture which manifested a quiet confidence and sense of higher service. The presentation examined the influence of both humanist classicism and Reformation piety in the works of Holbein. Saxl's method of approach joined the earlier inspirations of Dvořák and Wölfflin to his Warburgian perspective. Typical of Saxl, the lecture began with a caution, born most likely from his study with Wölfflin: "If we attempt to understand pictorial language, that is to say the language of forms, we always run the risk of weakening or frustrating our efforts by the use of general terms which kill all the finer shades."[112] At the same time, Saxl himself raised a broad, intellectual question about Holbein's works: "Do they reflect the spirit of Luther?"[113] The lecture at the *Kunsthalle* examined both the formal subtlety and spiritual background of Holbein's artwork, but with the aim of comprehending its emotional emphasis, or, in Saxl's words, "to divine the special shade of the emotional life of earlier epochs."[114]

Saxl carefully contrasted the woodcuts and illustrations which Holbein completed on behalf of Luther's cause to the Reformation polemics and prints which conjured images of demonic figures and portents. "Holbein," he concluded, "is everywhere committed to the clear and regular forms of the organic world, which knows no monsters; he transforms supernatural brilliance into natural light; he makes his adversaries look foolish but not ferocious."[115] Holbein produced "a singular synthesis"[116] of scriptural and classical traditions. His illustrations for Luther's translation of the Bible depicted needful, corruptible human beings, who yet exhibited an independence of movement and measure of self-awareness alien to Luther's message. Similarly, although Holbein's drawing of the isolated figure of Isaiah epitomized Luther's vision of humanity alone before God, the "restrained gesture"[117] of Holbein's prophet displayed an element foreign to Luther's holy passion. Holbein's art reflected his Erasmian sympathies. Indeed, his justly renowned portrait of Erasmus embodied Holbein's own ideals: "The sole object of the representation is the classical head of a modern personality alive with a sense of the dignity and power which are the gifts of a disciplined mind."[118] In Erasmus, classical learning united with Christian devotion: as Saxl explained, the Erasmian conviction that "each man's spiritual welfare is in his own hands and not the concern of social and religious authorities" expressed both the ancient belief in "the free movement of mind and body"[119] and the Reformers' call for inward piety. Holbein's work conveyed the vision of an artist who embraced the Erasmian union of Christianity and paganism, and who "wants his world to be free through humanism."[120]

From Saxl's perspective, Holbein's work represented a successful artistic and emotional synthesis: under the influence of a new pietism, art and scholarship had revived ancient models, and learned from those models how to exercise their own freedom. Perhaps the examples of Holbein and Erasmus reflected Saxl's own sense of purpose and expectation at the moment when the Warburg school had finally secured its brief interwar presence in the cultural life of Hamburg. Saxl, however, remained well aware of the difficulties in achieving the artistic and emotional integration accomplished by Holbein. In the winter term, 1930/31 he delivered at the university a lecture which explored those difficulties and which in certain respects served as a companion piece to the presentation on Holbein. The topic and mood of the lecture reflected the changing conditions brought by the depression and by the appearance of the Nazi menace.

Saxl's lecture examined the efforts by German artist Adam Elsheimer (1578–1610) to join Northern traditions in landscape painting to Italian, classical models.[121] Netherlandish and German traditions focused on human figures as part of a carefully delineated, richly detailed landscape, whereas Italian Renaissance art emphasized human freedom of movement and expression as the center of interest. Unifying those two opposing tendencies demanded of Elsheimer more than technical skill: a "moral effort was needed to make the attempt of combining North and South instead of thinking of them in terms of an 'either . . . or.' "[122] After emigrating to Italy as a young man, Elsheimer, like Holbein, worked out his first attempt at synthesis in the depiction of scripture, specifically the Holy Family's flight into Egypt (Figure 18). Applying Northern models, he pictured that a "perfect harmony reigns between man and landscape;"[123] at the same time, the painter "has learned to narrate biblical stories and to express the poetry of northern scenery by moonshine and torchlight in the even rhythms of classical language."[124] Elsheimer demonstrated his acquired mastery over the classical language in painting in his depiction of *Nymph and Satyr*, in which the two mythical figures exuded "an enchanting grace and a robust sensuality."[125] The nymph's inward gaze and "the clear soft rhythms of the landscape," however, began to betray "the melancholic key-note of Elsheimer's classical visions"[126] (Figure 19). The synthesis after which Elsheimer strove, and which he achieved only at great emotional cost to himself, emerged most fully not in biblical or mythological scenes but in his Italian landscapes. His painting of Tivoli with the ruins of the temple of the Sibyl embodied Elsheimer's Arcadian vision, an image of both a natural and classical utopia, in which "the elements of nature, trees, water, ruins, scenery and human beings are now subjected to such a lucid order that they become one with the unorganic shapes of classical architecture and statuary, originally foreign to northern taste. A new unity is born: the image of that dreamland Arcadia in which living things are disciplined without losing their fullness"[127] (Figure 20). The vision survived only briefly: Elsheimer died at thirty-one, never able to escape his own melancholia, his own inward sensation of loss. His search for unity in art reflected a personal, psychological battle: "He longs to find the artistic formula which will unite his own nature with everything that he admires in the South; he goes through a series of struggles and, after having reached a high stage of perfection, at last breaks down under the burden of his mission."[128]

Having placed Elsheimer's struggle before a university audience, Saxl concluded by reminding his listeners of the immediate significance of the painter's moral mission: "his burden is still being borne by our own generation, by each one of us."[129] The survival of Warburg's project in Hamburg, which had looked promising a few years earlier, had become doubtful. On a personal level Saxl's concluding remark raised the question as to whether his own rediscovery of antiquity could combat the sense of loss which now perhaps began to grow in him as it had once taken root in the painter Elsheimer.

In Holbein the revival of classical antiquity granted the vision of a world filled with a new spiritual freedom and self-discipline; in Elsheimer, it evoked the image of an Arcadia beyond reach. Both visions possessed pagan origins; both reappeared in medieval and Renaissance Europe with the revival of ancient astrology and its belief in the magic identity between man and the cosmos. As he explained in a Hamburg lecture, the ancient belief in an identity between microcosm and macrocosm—between the structure and movements of the human being, and the structure and movements of the cosmos—resurfaced at the end of the thirteenth century in images of the astrological influence of heavenly bodies on human activities and in handbooks detailing how to control that influence. In Saxl's words, the restoration of pagan astrology was "not the sign of a new superstition but an example of regressive evolution."[130] Astrology revived the ancient search for the principles of harmony between the self and the world. Renaissance artists preserved the classical pictures of that search yet expressed through such images a new understanding of inward freedom and isolation. Dürer's famous engraving of a dismal, meditative Saturn in

18. Adam Elsheimer, *Flight into Egypt*. Munich, Alte Pinakothek. Photo: Foto Marburg/Art Resource, New York.

Melencolia I resurrected a pagan formula to express a liberating but painful self-awareness: Dürer's "Melancholy is a symbol of the individual mind looking for its own image in the mirror of the universe."[131] The mind which thus discovered its own freedom became aware also of its own alienation. Leonardo confronted the same dilemma but instead perceived an equal necessity moving both the mind and the universe, a perception which elucidated "the miracle why in his drawings the visible world appears as an ordered whole and schematic constructions look like living organisms."[132]

The revival of antiquity, as Saxl described it in his Hamburg lectures, produced images which conveyed both a feeling of harmony between the

19. Adam Elsheimer, *Nymph and Satyr*. Berlin, Staatliche Museen. Photo: Foto Marburg/Art Resource, New York.

self and the world and an unrelieved sensation of loss or sense of dissociation from the world. The Warburg Library provided a secure location in which the once traveling scholar sought to comprehend both experiences and to chart the patterns—or rhythms—according to which they emerged in Renaissance art. In 1933, however, such contemplation and scholarship ceased to be possible in Hamburg. In April began the Nazi purge of Jewish university professors and officials; by the end of the year approximately twelve-hundred academics had been deprived of their positions.[133] Saxl did not wait for dismissal but resigned his honorary professorship from the University of Hamburg and looked to emigration. He hoped to find a new home abroad for the Warburg Library, but moving the institute rested with the decision of the Warburg brothers and remained subject to

20. Adam Elsheimer, *View of Tivoli*. Prague, National Gallery. Photo: National Gallery, Prague.

the hostility of the Nazi government. By the end of the summer Max Warburg finally agreed to transfer the library. At the insistence of Sir Denison Ross, director of the British School of Oriental Studies, a committee had formed to find refuge for Warburg's library in England. That committee, under the direction of Lord Lee of Fareham—chairman of the Courtauld Institute—presented to the Warburg family a proposal for moving the library to London. The offer came with a pledge of private financial support from Samuel Courtauld. In October Max Warburg accepted the plan. The local director of the Nazi Authority for Church and Artistic Matters in Hamburg only accepted the collection's transfer on the condition that the

Warburg family and the committee regarded the move as a temporary loan. In December 1933 the Warburg Library arrived in London, with a three-year reprieve from the Nazi government. As Hugh Lloyd-Jones wrote, "The transfer of the Library was effected only just in time. Not long after the books had been removed all decisions regarding emigration were transferred to the central party office in Berlin."[134] Years later Saxl commented to the *Manchester Guardian:* "Some scholars like Petrarch or Erasmus have always been fond of travelling, but travelling adventures are not so common in the lives of learned institutions."[135]

VII

Petrarch's travels became the starting point of one of Saxl's earliest series of lectures in his new home, lectures devoted specifically to the migration and survival of humanism in Venice. In three presentations delivered at the Warburg Library in London in 1935 Saxl examined the classical revival across two centuries of Venetian history, exploring through Venetian art various meanings of artistic renewal. Throughout the presentations Saxl sounded the theme which now recurred more strongly in his lectures: classicism received life in new places and times not only through the rediscovery of ancient models and revival of pagan emotions but through contact with contemporary images and impulses.

Saxl's examination of the rhythm of classical revival in Venice began with the time period of Petrarch's Venetian sojourn. The Florentine humanist's five-year stay in Venice during the 1360s coincided with the appearance in Venetian art of the realism and rounded sculptural approach characteristic of Tuscan works. That new naturalism and fullness in technique, rather than a resurrection of pagan formulas, inspired a Greek resurgence in Venice, and transformed the city-state's Christian Byzantine tradition: "the new achievement lies in the fact that by introducing strong realistic features, by making the figures more solid and the gestures more expressive, the old Byzantine style—in itself classical—is rejuvenated."[136] Regarding the influence of sculptural art, Saxl similarly emphasized "the new feeling for sculptural values, and sculpture in general, that tends of itself to revive the forms of classical antiquity."[137] Thus did contemporary Tuscan tendencies revitalize pagan artistic impulses in the maritime republic.

Following Petrarch's visit generations of Venetian artists began to explore the classical past for its own sake. That self-guided Venetian rediscovery of antiquity produced two distinct prototypes: Jacopo Bellini's mythological model and Mantegna's archeological example. While Bellini embodied the new antiquarian interest in Roman inscriptions, monuments, and statuary, the painter's own creative impulse expressed itself in the construction of mythic scenes—"great sentimental scenes *all'antica* which cannot be related to texts or marbles, but which interpret classical subjects in a new and highly subjective language."[138] Thus, in Bellini's art, Bacchic figures did not disintegrate into pagan abandonment but instead preserved an ancient sense of attachment to life. His figures of ancient mourners portrayed not a frenzy of grief but a meditation on death. In Bellini's case, "the gap between Christian and pagan feeling is bridged by the use of classical ideas for the formation of new allegories which in fact are accepted in a modern, that is a Christian, spirit."[139] In contrast to Bellini, Mantegna, who did not bring the classical into contact with the modern, deprived the ancients of a source of renewed life and movement: "Mantegna executes whole compositions in the spirit of Roman sculpture. Yet in doing so he gives them an antique character that is essentially unreal."[140] The classical world itself contained an antidote to that monumentalism and archeological severity: the skeptical, humanizing tradition within Greek poetry and philosophy which depicted the Olympian gods as part of the world of the "natural and commonplace,"[141] and which the Venetian, Giovanni Bellini, the son of Jacopo, revived in his own painting.

The process by which Venice revitalized ancient imagery and gathered within it a new sense of life and movement culminated with Titian. The Venetian master's early work depicted fragments of ancient sculpture and monuments not as relics of the past but as visual components of contemporary experience. As Saxl explained, "Titian is the first, so far as I can see, to look at classical marbles in the same spirit as we regard ruins of a remote age, that is, as monuments which, broken as they are, do not belong entirely to the past but are part of our living surroundings. He is no archaeologist, and therefore he does not try to restore them to the state in which they might have been centuries ago; he looks at them as he looks at the trees and plants and houses of his surroundings."[142] During that initial phase of his career, Titian treated not only marble fragments but also ancient figures themselves as contemporary realities. Titian's Uffizi Venus appeared not as a pagan revival but as a modern presence, a triumph of Venetian use of color and attention to the ordinary, which conferred on the scene of the goddess a natural atmosphere and sense of nearness: "in the Uffizi picture classical sculptural beauty seems to be overpowered by what one would like to call real life"[143] (Figure 21).

Titian's journey to Rome, where he directly encountered the surviving models of classical sculpture, infused his later work with a new paganism. Under the spell of his Roman sojourn, Titian turned to the re-creation of mythic scenes in their ancient intensity and meaning. As illustrated by his second portrait of Danae, the impact of such scenes derived both from the force of Titian's rediscovery of the past and from his own power of invention: "Firmly rooted in the natural soil of a classical country, he calls into being once again the great passionate scenes of ancient mythology, with no attempt at any slavish imitation of a model"[144] (Figure 22). To produce mimesis—to regenerate the fragment of a pagan drama—Titian applied the Venetian play with color to the lines of antique sculpture: "Titian's later picture of Danae is dramatic through the force of light and shade, which makes the figure of the reclining woman the only clear and quiet part amidst the uproar of the elements."[145] In that second Danae, however, color began also to serve yet another dramaturgic function—by dissolving well-defined, outward contours it gave expression to inward motive elements. Describing Danae's gaze, Saxl stated: "It is the expression of an emotion which touches the figure with momentary force, an expression opposed in its ambiguity to that conveyed by classical statuary; it is the expression of something indefinable and indefinite that moves behind the surface of a body still preserving the classical attitude."[146] Through new color and modeling Titian re-created the atmosphere of a stage action even in those later works in which "the drama lies only in the inner tension of the figures."[147] The evolution of his painting reflected a development which had occurred within ancient tragedy itself in the time

21. Titian, *Venus of Urbino*. Florence, Galleria degli Uffizi. Photo: Alinari/Art Resource, New York.

from Aeschylus to Euripides: having restored the presence of mythological objects, Titian ultimately depicted drama as the product of internal human conflicts and anguish. With his rediscovery of pagan images, Titian finally found those gestures of lamentation with which, in his last years, he portrayed not only the marks of human suffering but also his own redemptive search.

VIII

The development of Venetian art represented a steadily evolving rhythm —a rhythm expressed in journeying, in experiments with color, and in

22. Titian, *Danae and the Shower of Gold.* Madrid, Museo Nacional del Prado. Photo: Giraudon/Art Resource, New York.

modern transformations of ancient drama. In Saxl himself that rhythm perhaps manifested itself in what colleagues described as the stoical acceptance and perseverance with which he confronted the tasks imposed by exile and war.[148] The most pressing official task which confronted him when preparing the Venetian lectures in 1935—extending the stay of the Warburg Library in London—found resolution when a year later Samuel Courtauld offered the library his continued financial support and the University of London provided space for the institution in one of its own buildings. With a more secure institutional foundation, Saxl applied the resources of the library to answering wider demands of its time and place:

providing haven and work for exiled scholars, and integrating the library's efforts with the needs of British scholarship and the British public. He helped to found the new English-language *Journal of the Warburg Institute* and collaborated with the British Museum on an inventory of illuminated manuscripts. Before and during the war Saxl responded to the immediate crisis and the needs of a broader public by preserving a photographic record of structures endangered by bombing, and by sustaining popular education in the arts through photographic exhibitions which toured England. One of those exhibitions—a history of the contacts between Mediterranean and British art—became the subject of a book coauthored by Saxl and Rudolf Wittkower after the war.[149]

Not only in popular exhibitions but also in his own lectures Saxl recollected the cosmopolitan European tradition in art and science which dated to late antiquity and the Middle Ages, and which had collapsed on the continent in his own day. Saxl's presentation on English science manuscripts in 1938 traced how English monks who sojourned at the French Carolingian monastery of Fleury returned to the British isles with knowledge of ancient astronomical and astrological traditions preserved in France. His lectures on medieval encyclopedias charted the participation of French, English, Flemish, German, and south Italian monastic figures in the collection and illustration of knowledge from the end of the Roman world to the Renaissance.[150] The coming of war, however, also engendered thoughts on an entirely different rhythm of ancient revival—a rhythm within the artist, one which reached its culmination only at the close of life and which Rembrandt had exemplified in his portrait of Homer (Figure 23). Modeled on a Hellenistic bust of the ancient Greek poet, the painting depicted an inspired figure who endured great weariness: "In hellenistic sculpture the passion of the blind poet, the hollowness of his eyes, the wrinkles on his forehead, the burden of age were for the first time combined with the idea of the creative power of the poet who sang the Iliad and the Odyssey. This language of hellenism was accessible to the aging Rembrandt."[151] Saxl conjured his own image of the Dutch artist deprived of home and familiar objects: "we see the later Rembrandt who has left his house and sold his collection, and is now finally able to identify himself with the poet of the Iliad."[152]

23. Rembrandt van Rijn, *Homer*. The Hague, Mauritshuis. Photo: Scala/Art Resource, New York.

Saxl remained guardian of Aby Warburg's collection throughout the war, during which time he reflected not only upon the history of the ancient tradition on the continent but also upon the relationships between political power and artistic creativity. His lecture on Velázquez examined how the Spanish court painter preserved his creative autonomy despite the demands of court politics. Although a royal propagandist, Velázquez nonetheless conveyed his own vision of power moderated by human limitations, or as he depicted in the surrender at Breda, even capable of mercy. In the same spirit, Velázquez painted the Meninas as a monumental court scene rendered humanly familiar by the atmosphere of the artist's studio and the playfulness of the children.[153] In his lecture on the Vatican Appartamento Borgia of Pope Alexander VI, Saxl described a ruinous contrast to Velázquez's visions. Alexander VI selected as symbol of the Borgias and his papacy the image of the bull—a primitive, pagan image of fertility and ferocity which over the course of centuries had also come to embody among followers of ancient Mithraism and Christianity spiritual longing and regeneration. In Alexander's choice of the symbol of the bull, however, Saxl perceived not the rebirth of pagan antiquity in the Christian spirit, but an act of modern, political self-glorification: it was "symptomatic of Alexander, the dangerous Borgia character striving for power, not that he had the Appartamento decorated with a mixture of Christian and pagan subjects, but that he chose from the classical heritage the symbol of the bull, linking it up with the genealogy of his family which it was his constant endeavour to raise to ever greater power."[154] For Saxl—as for Kris—the modern political manipulation of images, which dated to the Renaissance and reached its fearsome apogee in the twentieth century, marked the danger which accompanied the revival of the ancient past.[155]

Yet, the contemporary European world produced artists who countered such manipulation, painters who remained true inheritors of the classical legacy even as they transformed or rebelled against it. Among such figures Saxl emphasized the example of Paul Cézanne, who revived the Venetian method of combining ancient and modern visions through the use of color. Of Cézanne's 1906 painting, *The Large Bathers*, Saxl stated: "There exists a much more subtle rhythm along with that of lines and shadows. It lies in the distribution of colours, which balance, modify, dissolve and unite the rhythm of forms"[156] (Figure 24). In Cézanne's images no opposition existed between individual freedom of movement and the universal pattern of natural creation: "Freedom and rhythm should no longer be contrasted but united in a world where colour has the power to merge them. In striving after such a world Cézanne is a true humanist. It is a humanism, no longer based on the details of classical learning, yet governed by the essential principles of the classical tradition."[157]

Saxl recalled Cézanne's achievement—the contemporary renewal of "the glorious Venetian tradition"[158]—in the month that the war in Europe came to an end. In 1948, for a lecture delivered shortly before he died, Saxl recollected still another form of contemporary humanism, embodied not in the colorful unification of fragments of nature but in a painful depiction of a world brutally returned to fragments—Picasso's *Guernica* (Figure 25). As Saxl reminded his listeners, *Guernica* portrayed the bombing of an innocent town eleven years earlier by German pilots who served the causes of Franco and fascism. Displayed at the Paris World Fair of 1937, "it will," Saxl maintained, "go down in history as one of the few great and prophetic works of art created between the wars."[159] Recalling the painting, Saxl remembered anew the haven which Fortune had granted him in London: "When one stood in front of it one sensed an atmosphere as tense and laden with cruelty as it then actually was, but as we others only acknowledged it to be in 1939 when war broke out."[160] In *Guernica* Picasso restored the formula of the bull to its primitive significance as a source of ferocious destruction. The émigré scholar described for his audience the scene depicted by Picasso: "The horse seems to hiss at the bull. It does not collapse although its body is pierced by a weapon. In its death agony it seems to vomit hatred. Two furious and despairing women are on the right, and in the centre is the distorted white head of the woman with the long arm above her head, her hand clutching the light which will make the deeds of the bull visible to the world."[161] The interpreter of ancient images asked his listeners to envision an art historian rediscovering *Guernica* three centuries after Picasso's day. Saxl, who for decades had traced the revival of the classical tradition but who also had in 1918 organized an antiwar photographic exhibition in Vienna, emphasized that the future observer had above all else to recognize in the ancient formulas the destruction

24. Paul Cézanne, *The Large Bathers.* Philadelphia Museum of Art: purchased with the W. P. Wilstach Fund. Photo: Philadelphia Museum of Art.

of a defenseless Basque town, and the immediate impact which the most powerful antifascist protest in contemporary art produced on thousands of spectators in 1937. Drawing attention to the danger which had begun to press upon postwar humanity, Saxl speculated that Picasso's painting might also educate a future art historian—and presumably Saxl's own listeners—on "the methods of warfare leading up to the atomic bomb."[162]

The commentary on *Guernica* demonstrated one of Saxl's strongest

25. Pablo Picasso, *Guernica*. Madrid, Museo Nacional Centro de Arte Reina Sofía. Photo: Giraudon/Art Resource, New York. © 2001 Estate of Pablo Picasso/Artists Rights Society, New York.

motivations for studying the revival of pagan antiquity: an intense interest in the artist's engagement with his own surroundings and historical period. Those artists whom Saxl greatly admired—Holbein, "his beloved Titian,"[163] Cézanne—conveyed through ancient fragments and models their own modern visions, impulses, and aspirations. Repeatedly reworking classical images, they illuminated their changing responses to their own worlds. Saxl recognized that such artists continuously redefined their images not only of the ancient past but also of the immediate present. Perhaps such a realization reflected the experience of a journeyman and exile.

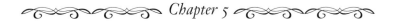

A Memory of Greece

I

In the memoir of his life before the Second World War, Kenneth Clark, British art historian and former director of the National Gallery, explained that "in this book I use the words 'I remember' only about episodes which I can still recall in movement, or which seem to cause a slight vibration in my mind."[1] Among the most vivid of such episodes Clark included his attendance in 1927 at Aby Warburg's final lecture in Rome, as a result of which the art student sojourning in Italy developed a permanent interest in images as symbols. Not only Warburg's ideas but the mode of presentation left an impression on Clark, who recalled of the Hamburg scholar:

> He himself said that if he had been five inches taller (he was even shorter than Berenson) he would have become an actor, and I can believe it, for he had, to an uncanny degree, the gift of mimesis. He could "get inside" a character, so that when he quoted from Savonarola, one seemed to hear the Frate's high, compelling voice; and when he read from Poliziano there was all the daintiness and the slight artificiality of the Medicean circle.[2]

In 1933, the year of his appointment to the directorship of the National Gallery, Clark played a not insignificant role in securing the survival of Warburg's legacy by encouraging Lord Lee of Fareham to seek a refuge for the Warburg Library in London.[3]

Clark's recollections of Warburg, and his own attitude toward memory, emphasized his own search for the quality of living movement in images. True to the Warburgian tradition, the British art historian understood images not only as visual depictions and mental pictures but also as dramatizations—in this example, Warburg's own enactment of absent Florentine figures. Not only Warburg and Clark but Freud too approached the study of art by endeavoring to answer how images came dramatically to life—how mimesis occurred. Like Warburg, Freud expanded his explorations of artistic creativity to include ritual enactment, perceiving in both painting and ritual recovered fragments of a primal tragedy. The revival of those fragments imparted a sense of movement to visual creations and ceremonial scenes.

As Kris and Saxl emphasized, the creation and enactment of images served not only to recover portions of the past but also to renew one's engagement with the world of the present. Kris's concept of enacted biography—the internalizing and acting out of typical images—connected the survival of images to lived as well as to staged drama. A student of Kris in Vienna, Erik Erikson later stressed dramatization as an essential process by which children and adolescents preserved and developed images of themselves and the world and expanded their contact with and mastery of external reality. While the process culminated with the young individual acquiring a self-defined image and role—an independent identity—mimesis continued to perform a necessary psychological function in the adult: "In the laboratory, on the stage, and on the drawing board, he relives the past and thus relieves leftover affects; in reconstructing the model situation, he redeems his failures and strengthens his hopes."[4] The postwar writer and theater critic Eric Bentley also stressed that individuals only understood themselves and others by acquiring dramatized images of human character, both on and off the stage: "We do not see others so much as certain substitutions for others. We do not see ourselves so much as others with whom we are identified."[5] So too Warburg dramatized his self-conceived identity as a Renaissance Florentine.

An enactment such as Warburg's associated itself closely with a particular place—in this instance, the city of Florence. Near the end of the Second World War, Saxl traced the Florentine connections in the lives of three émigré art historians, including his mentor. Saxl considered first the example of English artist and architect Herbert Horne, who authored a biography of Botticelli and approached Florence as an object of detached, aesthetic analysis. Horne abruptly broke with his past, departed England, and "became an austere Florentine scholar who rather shunned the company of men. His main interest in life was from then on to write on Botticelli accurately and disinterestedly, in a frigid style which almost obliterates the personality of the author."[6] For Warburg the Tuscan city provided a scene of drama and identification, and after his permanent return to Hamburg, he "never became quite reconciled to life in the Hansa town."[7] In the artwork and archives of Florence, Warburg followed the dynamics of the pagan renewal, determining upon that city as the location in which to explore "the question of survivals and revivals."[8] Saxl concluded his lecture with the example of Jacques Mesnil, the political sympathizer and friend of both the anarchist Elisée Reclus and of the pacifist and mystic Romain Rolland. Mesnil settled for a time in Tuscany, where he befriended Warburg. Like both Horne and Warburg, he wrote on Botticelli, as well as contributed volumes on Italy to Baedeker's travel guides.[9] Both Mesnil's politics and his interest in the art of Tuscany "sprang from a profound loathing of the ugliness, the injustices, the drift of contemporary life away from his ideal of goodwill and freedom."[10] Mesnil found in the Florentine Renaissance a model of "intellectual freedom and artistic awakening,"[11] and in the Tuscan peasant countryside an ideal of non-industrial civilization—and at least temporarily a new life and community for himself. In 1940, under the German occupation of Europe, Mesnil died in a French monastery, his last haven.

The three scholars' engagement with Florence and its environs reflected their attitudes toward history. In the case of Horne, who isolated himself from the world immediately around him in order to construct his own world of Florentine artifacts, "his mind was only directed towards the past."[12] For Warburg and Mesnil, however, the city and its Tuscan surroundings joined the life of the past to existence in the present. Indeed, Warburg's study of Florentine art and pagan imagery represented "his attempt at finding a common denominator for the past and the present."[13] In Mesnil's life and vision, Florence's history combined with the living countryside to produce a brief Tuscan Utopia. Thus did Saxl compose a Florentine triptych, whose panels displayed how a single place generated three processes of return.

II

Throughout the interwar years, Sigmund Freud maintained contact with Jacques Mesnil's friend, Romain Rolland, addressing his meditation on the future of human community—*Civilization and Its Discontents*—to the French writer. In 1936, on the occasion of Rolland's seventieth birthday, Freud composed an open letter to him, in which the psychoanalyst reflected upon the significance of place in our relationship to the past and present. The letter recounted a brief journey to Greece.

In the summer of 1904, Freud and his brother decided to visit Corfu, with Trieste as their departure point. An acquaintance in the Adriatic port city recommended, however, that they avoid Corfu at that time, and urged the travelers instead to sail for Athens. The recommendation to change plans put both him and his brother "in remarkably depressed spirits."[14] They perceived several obstacles to their embarking for Athens. Yet, at the moment of decision, they followed a nameless urge to visit the ancient city: "But when the time came, we went up to the counter and booked our passages for Athens as though it were a matter of course, without bothering in the least about the supposed difficulties and indeed without having discussed with one another the reasons for our decision."[15] On the day they reached Athens, Freud surveyed the surrounding landscape from the Acropolis and for an instant felt a sensation of doubt at the very existence of the ancient vicinity which he had first imagined in his schooldays and which he now saw for himself. As if he had never quite believed his classical instructors, the unusual idea occurred to the Viennese sojourner, " 'So all this really *does* exist, just as we learnt at school!' "[16]

Freud characterized his experience on the Acropolis as a disturbance of memory. In his youth Freud had not questioned the existence of the ancient location but only whether he would ever visit its precincts. A sensation of "derealization"[17]—the doubt as to the reality of the Acropolis ruins—had displaced itself onto his past, attaching itself to a memory of his early schooling in the classics. Freud interpreted the motive of that sense of derealization—and also of the depression which befell him in Trieste—as a feeling of guilt for his travels, for having gone beyond in those journeys the accomplishments of his father. "Thus," he explained to Rolland, "what interfered with our enjoyment of the journey to Athens was a feeling of *filial piety*. And now you will no longer wonder that the recollection of this incident on the Acropolis should have troubled me so often since I myself have grown old and stand in need of forebearance and can travel no more."[18] Freud wrote the letter to Rolland in January 1936; in June 1938, the *Anschluss* forced upon him a final journey to London.

Freud's visit to the Acropolis not only stirred memories of the past but produced in him a momentary feeling of inner detachment, which only years later he resolved fully. He finally retold and reexplored that mental experience at a time not only when the opportunity to travel to Athens had been lost to him because of age but also when the classical culture of which the Acropolis had been the focal point confronted its most dangerous threat. The letter to Rolland served to reclaim at that moment the psychological and cultural role which Athens had played in the life of the psychoanalyst and of Europe. Throughout centuries visitors had ceremonially approached the ancient site to rediscover remnants of antiquity and reexamine their own sense of engagement with the present. So too did Freud and Warburg, Kris and Saxl approach the work of art, exploring there how fragmented images of the past remained alive, and how estrangement from the present sought resolution.

Perhaps Freud's message to Rolland itself evidenced the afterlife of antiquity. Within the tale of Trieste and Greece there survived, in a highly reworked condition, traces of Aeschylus' drama of Orestes. A traveler undertook a journey impelled by a nameless necessity. That wordless compulsion generated within him an overwhelming sense of remoteness from the world, yet the same compelling force finally granted him restitution. From Athens the traveler embarked upon his return to the world. Images of dramatic necessity which dated to Aeschylus thus remained with Freud, images which persisted in fragments of his letter.

Notes

CHAPTER 1

1. Erik Barnouw, *Documentary: A History of the Non-Fiction Film* (London: Oxford University Press, 1974), 6. On Freud's first dream analysis, see Sigmund Freud to Wilhelm Fliess, 12 June 1900 and 18 June 1900, *The Complete Letters of Sigmund Freud to Wilhelm Fliess 1887–1904*, ed. and trans. Jeffrey Moussaieff Masson (Cambridge, Mass.: Harvard University Press, Belknap Press, 1985), 417–19.

2. See Barnouw, *Documentary*, 6. For a comparison of how the earliest filmmakers and how Warburg conceived of problems in depicting movement, see Philippe-Alain Michaud, *Aby Warburg et l'image en mouvement* (Paris: Éditions Macula, 1998), 43–64. Michaud likened the original studio-produced, kinetoscope images to dream hallucinations as described by Freud, in which temporal and spatial connections become transformed (ibid., 47). For a discussion of how various Post-Renaissance, especially northern European, techniques of painting, illustrating, and print reproduction influenced filmmaking, see Anne Hollander, *Moving Pictures* (Cambridge, Mass.: Harvard University Press, 1991), *passim*.

3. On Renoir's use of individual frames as independent images, see Alexander Sesonske, *Jean Renoir: The French Films, 1924–1939*, Harvard Film Studies (Cambridge, Mass.: Harvard University Press, 1980), xi, and André Bazin, *Jean Renoir*, ed. François Truffaut, trans. W. W. Halsey II and William H. Simon (New York: Dell Publishing, Delta Book, 1974), 146.

4. Jean Renoir, *An Interview* (København, Denmark: Green Integer Books, 1998), 32–33.

5. Ibid., 51–52. For the early influence of theater in Renoir's life, see Jean Renoir, *My Life and My Films*, trans. Norman Denny (New York: Atheneum, 1974), 29–30.

6. Jean Renoir, *Renoir, My Father*, trans. Randolph and Dorothy Weaver (Boston: Little, Brown, 1958), 221.

7. For comparison of Burckhardt's own conception of art history as a branch of psychology to that of Lamprecht, see E. H. Gombrich, *Aby Warburg: An Intellectual Biography*, 2d ed. (Chicago: University of Chicago Press, 1986), 33–37; and Kurt

W. Forster, introduction to *The Renewal of Pagan Antiquity: Contributions to the Cultural History of the European Renaissance*, by Aby Warburg (Los Angeles: Getty Research Institute for the History of Art and the Humanities, 1999), 6–11.

8. G.E. Lessing, *Laocoon or On the Limits of Painting and Poetry* (1766), trans. William A. Steel and rev. H. B. Nisbet, in *German Aesthetic and Literary Criticism: Winckelmann, Lessing, Hamann, Herder, Schiller, Goethe*, ed. H. B. Nisbet (Cambridge: Cambridge University Press, 1985), 69.

9. Ibid., 99.

10. Ibid., 119.

11. Ibid. For an analysis of Lessing's conception of grace and the limits of painting, see Rensselaer W. Lee, *Ut Pictura Poesis: The Humanistic Theory of Painting* (New York: W. W. Norton, 1967), 20–23, 66. As if meditating on Lessing's argument on the distinction between poetry and painting, Primo Levi wrote a cautionary, but sympathetic account of Manzoni's unsuccessful efforts in *The Betrothed* at creating accurate literary depictions of physical gestures. See Primo Levi, "Renzo's Fist," in *Other People's Trades*, trans. Raymond Rosenthal (London: Abacus, 1991), 135–140.

12. Remaining religiously observant, Jacob Bernays pursued a highly distinguished career as a classical scholar. Because of his refusal to convert, university faculty positions became closed to him. The University of Bonn finally appointed him as a professor *Extraordinarius*, denying him a full chair because of his Judaism. For a discussion of the work of Isaak Bernays and Jacob Bernays, see Arnaldo Momigliano, "Jacob Bernays" (1969), in *A.D. Momigliano: Studies on Modern Scholarship*, ed. G.W. Bowersock and T.J. Cornell, trans. T. J. Cornell (Berkeley and Los Angeles: University of California Press, 1994), 121–46. In a letter to Arnold Zweig in 1932, Freud, who rendered some assistance in editing Jacob Bernays's correspondence for publication, referred to the ancient scholar as an "outstanding personality." See Sigmund Freud to Arnold Zweig, 27 Nov. 1932, *The Letters of Sigmund Freud and Arnold Zweig*, ed. Ernst L. Freud, trans. Elaine and William Robson-Scott (New York: Harcourt Brace Jovanovich, Helen and Kurt Wolff Book, 1970), 48. As Yosef Hayim Yerushalmi pointed out, Freud's letter to Zweig noted especially Jacob Bernays's refusal of conversion. See Yosef Hayim Yerushalmi, *Freud's Moses: Judaism Terminable and Interminable* (New Haven: Yale University Press, 1991), 47–48. Jacob Bernays died in 1881, the year before Freud met his future wife. No references to Jacob Bernays appear in Freud's published works.

13. Sigmund Freud to Martha Bernays, 23 July 1882, *The Letters of Sigmund Freud*, ed. Ernst L. Freud, trans. Tania and James Stern (New York: Basic Books, 1960), 21.

14. On Freud's ambivalent identification with the figure of Michelangelo's Moses, see Yerushalmi, *Freud's Moses*, 75–76; and Carl E. Schorske, "To the Egyptian

Dig: Freud's Psycho-Archeology of Cultures," in *Thinking With History: Explorations in the Passage to Modernism* (Princeton: Princeton University Press, 1998), 203–4.

15. Sigmund Freud, *Jokes and their Relation to the Unconscious* (1905), in *The Standard Edition of the Complete Psychological Works of Sigmund Freud*, translated from the German under the general editorship of James Strachey, in collaboration with Anna Freud, assisted by Alix Strachey and Alan Tyson (London: Hogarth Press and the Institute of Psycho-Analysis, 1953–74), 8: 92. For the quotation from act 4, scene 4 of Lessing's drama, see G.E. Lessing, *Nathan the Wise* (1779), trans. William A. Steel, in *Laocoön, Nathan the Wise, Minna von Barnhelm*, ed. William A. Steel (London: J.M. Dent and Sons, 1930, 1961), 189. When in 1934 Joseph Wortis asked Freud to name the authors who most influenced the psychoanalyst's prose style, Freud responded, " 'My conscious and deliberate model was Lessing.' " See Joseph Wortis, *Fragments of an Analysis with Freud* (New York: McGraw-Hill, 1975), 109. For specific influences of Lessing's Laocoon essay on the style and organization of Freud's prose, see Walter Schönau, *Sigmund Freuds Prosa: Literarische Elemente seines Stils* (Stuttgart: J. B. Metzlersche Verlagsbuchhandlung, 1968), 42–44.

16. See Felix Gilbert, "From Art History to the History of Civilization: Aby Warburg" (1972), review of *Aby Warburg: An Intellectual Biography*, by E.H. Gombrich, in *History: Choice and Commitment* (Cambridge, Mass.: Harvard University Press, Belknap Press, 1977), 436–37.

17. See A. M. Meyer, "Aby Warburg in His Early Correspondence," *American Scholar* 57 (Summer 1988): 452.

18. For Warburg's identification with the patrician class of Renaissance Florence, see for example Gilbert, "From Art History to the History of Civilization," 437, and Meyer, "Aby Warburg in His Early Correspondence," 445–46.

19. Fritz Saxl, "Three 'Florentines': Herbert Horne, A. Warburg, Jacques Mesnil" (1944), in *Lectures* (London: The Warburg Institute, University of London, 1957), 1: 336.

20. Ibid., 336.

21. Ernst Cassirer, *The Philosophy of the Enlightenment*, trans. Fritz C. A. Koelln and James B. Pettegrove (Princeton: Princeton University Press, 1951), 359.

22. Ibid., 360.

23. See E. M. Butler, *The Tyranny of Greece over Germany: A Study of the Influence Exercised by Greek Art and Poetry over the Great German Writers of the Eighteenth, Nineteenth, and Twentieth Centuries* (Cambridge: Cambridge University Press, 1935), 56–70.

24. Edgar Wind, "Warburg's Concept of *Kulturwissenschaft* and its Meaning for Aesthetics" (1930), in *The Eloquence of Symbols: Studies in Humanist Art*, ed. Jaynie Anderson, rev. ed. (Oxford: Clarendon Press, 1993), 26.

25. As Yerushalmi indicated, the conclusion of *Nathan the Wise* has received diverse applications. Freud's friend and colleague, the Swiss pastor, Oskar Pfister, interpreted it as embodying an open and unifying Christianity. Placing the work within its Enlightenment context, Yerushalmi more accurately identified the play as Lessing's "glowing testimony to his friendship with Moses Mendelssohn and a singular document of a moment when the future seemed full of promise for German-Jewish brotherhood in a mutual religion of tolerant reason." See Yerushalmi, *Freud's Moses*, 8. Yerushalmi wrote of Freud that "a vital part of him lived in a Germanic universe of thought, but this Germany of the mind and the imagination that he, like so many other Central European Jews, cherished was that of the German Enlightenment, of *Nathan the Wise* (Pfister as Lessing-Saladin, Freud as Mendelssohn-Nathan), of literature and philosophy, of nineteenth-century German science" (Yerushalmi, *Freud's Moses*, 40). Charlotte Schoell-Glass emphasized that both Warburg and Freud intended their work to contribute to a revival of a movement toward intellectual and moral emancipation: "Warburg's concept of a cultural science can be interpreted as an attempt at a second Enlightenment—in this way also comparable with Freud's project—whose necessity for him followed from his personal and early experience of anti-Semitism, which resisted all enlightenment." Charlotte Schoell-Glass, *Aby Warburg und der Antisemitismus: Kulturwissenschaft als Geistespolitik* (Frankfurt am Main: Fischer Taschenbuch Verlag, 1998), 25. Most recently, Ritchie Robertson stressed that the representatives of the three religions in *Nathan the Wise* accepted each other not because they tolerated diverse religious observances, but because they rejected them in favor of a common, enlightened morality. Further, as Robertson pointed out, only Nathan did not share a direct blood relation to the other characters, thus evidencing his still tenuous position within the community—a position which Lessing did not resolve, but with which he perhaps felt some sympathy. See Ritchie Robertson, *The "Jewish Question" in German Literature 1749–1939: Emancipation and Its Discontents* (Oxford: Oxford University Press, 1999), 32–45. Translations are my own unless indicated otherwise.

26. Louis Rose, *The Freudian Calling: Early Viennese Psychoanalysis and the Pursuit of Cultural Science* (Detroit: Wayne State University Press, 1998), *passim*.

27. See for example Horst Bredekamp, " 'Du lebst und thust mir nichts': Anmerkungen zur Aktualität Aby Warburgs," in *Aby Warburg: Akten des internationalen Symposions Hamburg 1990*, ed. Horst Bredekamp, Michael Diers, and Charlotte Schoell-Glass (Weinheim: VCH, Act Humaniora, 1991), 2–3; Konrad Hoffmann, "Angst und Methode nach Warburg: Erinnerung als Veränderung," in *Aby Warburg: Akten*, ed. Bredekamp, Diers, and Schoell-Glass, 266; Margaret Iversen, "Retrieving Warburg's Tradition," *Art History* 16, no. 4 (Dec. 1993): 544–45; and Kurt W. Forster, "Aby Warburg: His Study of Ritual and Art on

Two Continents," *October* 77 (Summer 1996): 15. Most recently, Richard Brilliant wrote that "Aby Warburg certainly believed in the ghosts of the classical past and sought out the traces of antiquity in Renaissance pictorial imagery, as a detective or a psychoanalyst might seek out the visible clues that reveal actions taken or beliefs held." See Richard Brilliant, "Winckelmann and Warburg: Contrasting Attitudes toward the Instrumental Authority of Ancient Art," in *Antiquity and Its Interpreters*, ed. Alina Payne, Ann Kuttner, and Rebekah Smick (Cambridge: Cambridge University Press, 2000), 271–72. For an examination of the application of psychoanalysis to art historical studies, see Laurie Schneider Adams, *Art and Psychoanalysis* (New York: HarperCollins Publishers, Icon Editions, 1993), *passim*.

28. Fritz Saxl, "Elsheimer and Italy" (1930/31), in *Lectures*, 1: 296.

29. Fritz Saxl, "The Belief in Stars in the Twelfth Century" (1929/30), in *Lectures*, 1: 90.

30. Ibid., 91.

31. Fritz Saxl, "Titian and Pietro Aretino" (1935), in *Lectures:* 1, 173. In an article on classical inscriptions Saxl wrote: "It is, however, astonishing to realize how little interest 19th century philologists took in the personalities of their Renaissance predecessors. They mattered to them only in so far as they faithfully copied genuine classical texts. Why they copied the texts, what selections they made, what personal use they made of the material—these were no problems for the 19th century epigraphists. I think that a more psychological approach to the history of epigraphy is more in keeping with our general outlook, and that the result of such an attempt might yield a modest supplement to the achievements of 19th century scholarship." See Fritz Saxl, "The Classical Inscription in Renaissance Art and Politics," *Journal of the Warburg and Courtauld Institutes* 4, nos. 1 and 2 (Oct.-Jan. 1940–41): 20.

32. Sigmund Freud to Ludwig Binswanger, 3 Nov. 1921, quoted in Ron Chernow, *The Warburgs: The Twentieth-Century Odyssey of a Remarkable Jewish Family* (New York: Random House, 1993), 260.

33. See Gombrich, *Aby Warburg*, 184.

34. Warburg derived the term, *"das Nachleben der Antike"* from the German art historian, Anton Springer. See Gombrich, *Aby Warburg*, 49.

35. Horst Bredekamp, "'Du lebst und thust mir nichts': Anmerkungen zur Aktualität Aby Warburgs," in *Aby Warburg: Akten*, ed. Bredekamp, Diers, and Schoell-Glass, 2.

36. Fritz Saxl, "Why Art History?" (1948) in *Lectures*, 1: 346.

37. See Erich Auerbach, *Mimesis: The Representation of Reality in Western Literature*, trans. Willard R. Trask (Princeton: Princeton University Press, 1953), 3–23.

38. Ibid., 459.

39. Ibid., 465.

40. Ibid., 466.
41. Lessing, *Laocoon or On the Limits of Painting and Poetry*, 119.
42. Ibid., 58.
43. Jean-Pierre Vernant, "The Tragic Subject: Historicity and Transhistoricity," in Jean-Pierre Vernant and Pierre Vidal-Naquet, *Myth and Tragedy in Ancient Greece*, trans. Janet Lloyd (New York: Zone Books, 1990), 242.
44. Ibid., 243.
45. Ibid.
46. See Gerald F. Else, *The Origin and Early Form of Greek Tragedy* (New York: W. W. Norton, 1972), 48–55.
47. Jean-Pierre Vernant, "The Birth of Images," trans. Froma I. Zeitlin, in *Mortals and Immortals: Collected Essays*, ed. Froma I. Zeitlin (Princeton: Princeton University Press, 1991), 166.
48. Ibid.
49. Vernant wrote that the ancient dynamic reappeared with the invention of the cinema and the first experiences of filmgoers: "Totally unaccustomed to it, as they were, and not having had time to develop what might be called a consciousness of fiction or a way of reacting to the imaginary, they would boo the villains and cheer on and applaud the good guys on the screen, as if the shadows flickering there were living beings of flesh and blood; they mistook the spectacle for reality. The second response is to enter into the game, understanding that what can be seen on the stage belongs not to the plane of reality, but to what must be defined as the plane of theatrical illusion" (Vernant, "Tragic Subject," 243–44).
50. For a critical evaluation of the Cambridge circle as classical anthropologists, see M. I. Finley, "Anthropology and the Classics" (1972), in *The Use and Abuse of History* (London: Penguin Books, 1990), 102–19. For a recent reexamination of the origins, development, and reception of the Cambridge school of thought, see Robert Ackerman, *The Myth and Ritual School: J. G. Frazer and the Cambridge Ritualists* (New York: Garland, 1991), *passim*, and William M. Calder III, ed., *The Cambridge Ritualists Reconsidered* (Atlanta: Scholars Press, 1991), *passim*. Both books include a consideration of the work of William Robertson Smith, whose interpretation of totemism greatly influenced Freud, as will be discussed below.
51. Jane Ellen Harrison, *Ancient Art and Ritual* (New York: Henry Holt, 1913), 47.
52. Ibid., 129.
53. Ibid., 186.
54. Ibid., 197.
55. Ibid., 231.
56. See Francis M. Cornford, *Thucydides Mythistoricus* (Philadelphia: University of Pennsylvania Press, 1971), 221–43.

CHAPTER 2

1. Fritz Saxl, "The History of Warburg's Library (1886–1944)," in E. H. Gombrich, *Aby Warburg*, 327. On the creation and evolution of the library during Warburg's lifetime, see ibid., 325–28; Gombrich, *Aby Warburg*, 129–32; Chernow, *Warburgs*, 63–64, 117–21, 175, 195, 255–58, 263–66, 285–87; David Farrer, *The Warburgs: The Story of a Family* (New York: Stein and Day, 1974), 128–29; and Gertrud Bing, "Fritz Saxl (1890–1948): A Memoir," in *Fritz Saxl 1890–1948: A Volume of Memorial Essays from His Friends in England*, ed. D. J. Gordon (London: Thomas Nelson and Sons, 1957), 1–18. On the connections between the work of Panofsky and Cassirer and that of Warburg and Saxl, see Silvia Ferretti, *Cassirer, Panofsky, and Warburg: Symbol, Art, and History*, trans. Richard Pierce (New Haven: Yale University Press, 1989), *passim*; Carlo Ginzburg, "From Aby Warburg to E. H. Gombrich: A Problem of Method," in *Clues, Myth, and the Historical Method*, trans. John and Anne Tedeschi (Baltimore: Johns Hopkins University Press, 1989), 17–41; and Michael Ann Holly, *Panofsky and the Foundations of Art History* (Ithaca, N.Y.: Cornell University Press, 1984), 105–13. On Warburg's position within wider German academic society and scholarship, see Gilbert, "From Art History to the History of Civilization," 431–39.
2. Sigmund Freud, *The Interpretation of Dreams* (1900), in *Standard Edition*, 4: 314.
3. Ibid., 314.
4. According to Jean-Pierre Cuzin, the room's "function as a library is confirmed by the bases for cabinets . . . which were probably intended to support cupboards for books." See Jean-Pierre Cuzin, *Raphael: His Life and Works*, translated by Sarah Brown (Secaucus, N.J.: Chartwell Books, 1985), 103. Gombrich, it may be noted, expressed his doubts that the room served as a papal library. Further, he emphasized that the central meaning of its cycle of frescoes—the divine origin and nature of knowledge, virtue, and beauty—did not require that all of the figures of philosophers and poets be identified with persons from centuries past. See E.H. Gombrich, "Raphael's *Stanza della Segnatura* and the Nature of its Symbolism," in *Symbolic Images*, 3d ed. (London: Phaidon Press, 1985), 85–101.
5. Kurt W. Forster perceived in the organization of the library Warburg's effort to create a ritual surrounding capable of renewing thought associations. See Forster, "Aby Warburg: His Study of Ritual and Art on Two Continents," 9–12. For a discussion of the visual organization of collections as a guide to inquiry and knowledge, see Horst Bredekamp, *The Lure of Antiquity and the Cult of the Machine: The Kunstkammer and the Evolution of Nature, Art and Technology*, trans. Allison Brown (Princeton: Markus Wiener, 1995), 30–36.

6. Gombrich, *Aby Warburg*, 321. More recently, Margaret Iversen also suggested that Warburg and Freud possessed a similar worldview, but as critics of rational detachment. See Iversen, "Retrieving Warburg's Tradition," 541–53.

7. Aby Warburg, "Sandro Botticelli's *Birth of Venus* and *Spring*: An Examination of the Concepts of Antiquity in the Italian Early Renaissance" (1893), in *The Renewal of Pagan Antiquity: Contributions to the Cultural History of the European Renaissance*, trans. David Britt, Getty Research Institute Publications Programs: Texts and Documents (Los Angeles: Getty Research Institute for the History of Art and the Humanities, 1999), 110.

8. Gombrich, *Aby Warburg*, 56.

9. Warburg, "Sandro Botticelli's *Birth of Venus* and *Spring*," in *Renewal of Pagan Antiquity*, 95.

10. Ibid., 108.

11. Ibid., 125.

12. Gombrich, *Aby Warburg*, 63. In a recent essay Matthew Rampley explored links between the Romantic idea of empathy and Warburg's concept of mimesis. In the Romantic view, art elicited empathic feeling through the indication of movement. See Matthew Rampley, "From Symbol to Allegory: Aby Warburg's Theory of Art," *Art Bulletin* 79, no. 1 (Mar. 1997): 41–55.

13. Warburg, "Sandro Botticelli's *Birth of Venus* and *Spring*," in *Renewal of Pagan Antiquity*, 137.

14. Ibid., 139.

15. Ibid., 141.

16. Ibid., 96.

17. Aby Warburg, "Dürer and Italian Antiquity" (1905), in *Renewal of Pagan Antiquity*, 553.

18. Ibid.

19. Ibid., 555.

20. Ibid.

21. Ibid.

22. Ibid., 556.

23. Ibid., 558. For a comparison between Warburg's study of ancient pathos formulas and Jean Martin Charcot's nearly contemporaneous effort to record and codify the body language of hysterical patients, see Sigrid Schade, "Charcot and the Spectacle of the Hysterical Body: The 'Pathos Formula' as an Aesthetic Staging of Psychiatric Discourse—a Blind Spot in the Reception of Warburg," *Art History* 18, no. 4 (Dec. 1995): 499–517.

24. Aby Warburg, "Francesco Sassetti's Last Injunctions to His Sons" (1907), in *Renewal of Pagan Antiquity*, 240.

25. Ibid., 241.

26. Ibid.

27. Ibid., 240.
28. Ibid., 245.
29. Ibid.
30. Ibid.
31. Ibid., 247.
32. Ibid., 249.
33. Aby Warburg, "The Art of Portraiture and the Florentine Bourgeoisie: Domenico Ghirlandaio in Santa Trinita: The Portraits of Lorenzo de' Medici and His Household" (1902), in *Renewal of Pagan Antiquity*, 203. Sassetti and Lorenzo stand next to each other, with raised hands, furthest to the right in the foreground.
34. Ibid. According to Philippe-Alain Michaud, Ghirlandaio's frescoes created "a theatrical space intermediate between the universe of the city and that of rituals" (Michaud, *Aby Warburg et l'image en mouvement*, 119). The painting of the confirmation provided "a stage on which unfolds the spectacle of Sassetti's transfiguration" (ibid.).
35. Gombrich, *Aby Warburg*, 165.
36. Ibid., 175.
37. Warburg, "Francesco Sassetti's Last Injunctions to His Sons," 249.
38. Lessing, *Laocoon or On the Limits of Painting and Poetry*, 98.
39. Bernd Roeck, "Psychohistorie im Zeichen Saturns: Aby Warburgs Denksystem und die moderne Kulturgeschichte," in *Kulturgeschichte Heute*, ed. Wolfgang Hardtwig and Hans-Ulrich Wehler (Göttingen: Vandenhoeck & Ruprecht, 1996), 246.
40. Aby Warburg, "Italian Art and International Astrology in the Palazzo Schifanoia, Ferrara" (1912), in *Renewal of Pagan Antiquity*, 577.
41. Ibid., 565.
42. Ibid., 585.
43. Ibid.
44. Ibid.
45. Ibid., 586.
46. Ibid.
47. Warburg delivered the lecture at the Kreuzlingen clinic as a demonstration to his psychiatrist, Ludwig Binswinger, that he could return to his life and career in Hamburg. On the relationship between the scholarly and therapeutic aims of the presentation, see Michael P. Steinberg, "Aby Warburg's Kreuzlingen Lecture: A Reading," in *Images from the Region of the Pueblo Indians of North America*, by Aby Warburg (Ithaca, N.Y.: Cornell University Press, 1995), 70–73.
48. Aby Warburg, *Images from the Region of the Pueblo Indians of North America*, trans. Michael P. Steinberg (Ithaca, N.Y.: Cornell University Press, 1995), 34.
49. Ibid.

50. For a description and analysis of the Pueblo *kachina* rituals, see Armin W. Geertz, "Pueblo Cultural History," in *Photographs at the Frontier: Aby Warburg in America 1895–1896*, ed. Benedetta Cestelli Guidi and Nicholas Mann (London: Merrell Holberton, The Warburg Institute, 1998), 16–18. For an extensive selection from the photographic record which Warburg kept from his trip to New Mexico and Arizona, including dancers performing within community plazas and spectators seated on the roofs of houses, see "Catalogue of Aby Warburg's Photographs," in *Photographs at the Frontier*, 75–155. As Salvatore Settis explained, Warburg interpreted the afterlife of antiquity as a cultural phase experienced by Pueblo, as well as European societies, a phase which in both cases followed pagan beginnings and a Christian intermezzo. See Salvatore Settis, "Kunstgeschichte als vergleichende Kulturwissenschaft: Aby Warburg, die Pueblo-Indianer und das Nachleben der Antike," in *Künstlerischer Austausch Artistic Exchange: Akten des XXVIII. Internationalen Kongresses für Kunstgeschichte*, ed. Thomas W. Gaehtgens (Berlin: Akademie Verlag, 1993), 1: 146. Philippe-Alain Michaud described how Pueblo ritual dance also would have embodied for Warburg aspects of the Florentine ducal wedding festival of 1589. See Philippe-Alain Michaud, "Florence in New Mexico: The Intermezzi of 1589 in the Light of Indian Rituals," in *Photographs at the Frontier*, ed. Guidi and Mann, 53–63.

51. Warburg hoped that the Mennonite missionary Henry R. Voth in whose company he had viewed the *kachina* ritual would contribute a commentary on the Pueblo snake dance, the enactment of which Warburg had not observed on his journey. Voth declined, and Warburg composed no commentary on the *kachina* ritual until his Kreuzlingen lecture, which at Saxl's suggestion also included a focus on the snake dance. See Benedetta Cestelli Guidi, "Retracing Aby Warburg's American Journey through his Photographs," in *Photographs at the Frontier*, ed. Guidi and Mann, 34, 42.

52. Warburg, *Images from the Region of the Pueblo Indians of North America*, 2.

53. Ibid., 3.

54. Ibid., 16–17.

55. Ibid., 19.

56. As Jean-Pierre Vernant wrote, the ancient Greeks also recognized in the wearing of masks the danger of losing oneself to the other. The process of becoming the other in ritual and drama occurred within the realm of Dionysos, the god of masks: "The whole point of Dionysism, which brings man into immediate contact with the otherness of the divine, is to become other oneself, swinging into the gaze of the god or becoming assimilated to him through mimetic contagion." Jean-Pierre Vernant and Françoise Frontisi-Ducroux, "Features of the Mask in Ancient Greece," in Vernant and Vidal-Naquet, *Myth and Tragedy in Ancient Greece*, 204.

57. Warburg, *Images from the Region of the Pueblo Indians of North America*, 32.
58. Ibid., 35.
59. Ibid., 36.
60. Ibid., 44.
61. Ibid., 48.
62. Ibid.
63. Ibid.
64. Ibid., 38.
65. Ibid., 39.
66. Ibid., 52–53.
67. See Gombrich, *Aby Warburg*, 220, 224–26.
68. Ibid., 218.
69. Warburg discussed contrasting applications of pathos formulas in his lecture on Rembrandt, delivered in May 1926. See ibid., 229–38.
70. Aby Warburg, notes to *Mnemosyne*, quoted in ibid., 289.
71. Warburg, notes to *Mnemosyne*, quoted in ibid., 289.
72. Gombrich, *Aby Warburg*, 302.
73. E. H. Gombrich, *Art and Illusion: A Study in the Psychology of Pictorial Representation*, The A. W. Mellon Lectures in the Fine Arts, 1956, Bollingen Series (Princeton: Princeton University Press, 1969), 23.
74. See Ernest Jones, *The Life and Work of Sigmund Freud*, vol. 2 (New York: Basic Books, 1955), 384; and vol. 3 (New York: Basic Books, 1957), 86.
75. See Harald Wolf, "Emanuel Löwy: Leben und Werk eines vergessenen Pioniers," in *Emanuel Löwy: Ein vergessener Pionier*, ed. Friedrich Brien, Kataloge der Archäologischen Sammlung der Universität Wien, Sonderheft 1 (Vienna: Verlag des Clubs der Universität Wien, 1998), 15, 21.
76. Ibid., 33–34, 41, 44–45.
77. Emanuel Loewy, *The Rendering of Nature in Early Greek Art*, trans. John Fothergill (London: Duckworth, 1907), 10.
78. Ibid., 13.
79. Ibid., 12.
80. Ibid., 15.
81. Ibid.
82. Ibid., 16.
83. Ibid., 16–17.
84. Ibid., 17.
85. Ibid., 18.
86. Ibid., 19.
87. Ibid., 26.
88. Ibid., 27.

89. Ibid., 52.
90. Ibid., 78.
91. Ibid., 69.
92. Ibid., 20.
93. Ibid., 103.
94. Arnold Hauser, *The Social History of Art*, vol. 1, *Prehistoric Times, Ancient-Oriental Urban Cultures, Greece and Rome, The Middle Ages* (New York: Vintage Books, 1951), 76.
95. Loewy, *Rendering of Nature in Early Greek Art*, 79.
96. See Else, *Origin and Early Form of Greek Tragedy*, 86–87, 96.
97. Emanuel Loewy, "Ursprünge der bildenden Kunst," *Almanach der Akademie der Wissenschaften in Wien* 80 (1930): 277.
98. Ibid., 278.
99. Ibid., 293.
100. Ibid., 295.
101. Loewy, *Rendering of Nature in Early Greek Art*, 40.

CHAPTER 3

1. Freud's publisher attached the publication date 1900 to the book, which he in fact first issued in November 1899. See Ernest Jones, *The Life and Work of Sigmund Freud*, vol. 1 (New York: Basic Books, 1953), 360.
2. Freud, *Jokes and their Relation to the Unconscious*, 192.
3. Freud to Fliess, 6 Dec. 1896, *Complete Letters of Sigmund Freud to Wilhelm Fliess*, 214.
4. Freud, *Interpretation of Dreams*, 5: 340.
5. Ibid., 4: 283.
6. Ibid., 307–8. On transference, see also 5: 562. Saul Friedländer described the Freudian emphasis on the convergence, or overdetermination, of causal chains as contributing not only to a science of the mind but also to the study of history. See Saul Friedländer, *History and Psychoanalysis: An Inquiry into the Possibilities and Limits of Psychohistory*, trans. Susan Suleiman (New York: Holmes and Meier, 1978), 22–23.
7. Freud, *Interpretation of Dreams*, 4: 50. Jean-François Lyotard described the dream-work as the staging or "the mise-en-scène" that transcribed desires into movements and into emotions experienced bodily. Lyotard, however, questioned the possibility of any successful stage representation of desire. See Jean-François Lyotard, "The Unconscious as Mise-en-Scène" (1977), trans. Joseph Maier, in *Mimesis, Masochism, and Mime: The Politics of Theatricality in Contemporary French Thought*, ed. Timothy Murray (Ann Arbor: University of Michi-

gan Press, 1997), 163–174. On Freud's insight into the dramatizing tendencies within dreams as a product of his literary background, see Graham Frankland, *Freud's Literary Culture* (Cambridge: Cambridge University Press, 2000), 131.

8. Freud, *Interpretation of Dreams*, 5: 534.
9. Ibid., 538.
10. Ibid., 543.
11. Ibid., 546.
12. Ibid., 543.
13. Ibid., 553.
14. Ibid., 601.
15. Ibid., 605.
16. Ibid., 601.
17. Ibid., 605.
18. Ibid.
19. Jacques Lecoq, "Theatre of Gesture and Image," trans. Shelley Tepperman, in *The Intercultural Performance Reader*, ed. Patrice Pavis (London: Routledge, 1996), 141.
20. Freud, *Jokes and their Relation to the Unconscious*, 94.
21. Ibid., 101.
22. Ibid., 103.
23. Ibid., 118.
24. Ibid., 120.
25. Ibid., 166.
26. Karl Kraus, *Die Fackel* 9, no. 229 (2 July 1907): 4.
27. Freud, *Jokes and their Relation to the Unconscious*, 192.
28. Ibid., 193.
29. Ibid.
30. For a discussion of Freud's theory of ideational mimetics in relation to aesthetic theory at the turn of the century, see Jack J. Spector, *The Aesthetics of Freud: A Study in Psychoanalysis and Art* (New York: McGraw-Hill, 1974), 119–25.
31. Freud, *Jokes and Their Relation to the Unconscious*, 190.
32. Ibid., 191.
33. Ibid., 192.
34. Ibid., 194.
35. Sigmund Freud, *Delusions and Dreams in Jensen's "Gradiva"* (1907), in *Standard Edition*, 9: 8.
36. Ibid., 7.
37. Wilhelm Jensen, "Gradiva: A Pompeiian Fancy," trans. Helen M. Downey, in Sigmund Freud, *Delusion and Dreams and Other Essays*, ed. Philip Reiff (Boston: Beacon Press, 1956), 147–48. For the sake of consistency, I have referred to the

subtitle of Jensen's story within the text as "A Pompeian Fantasy," the translation which appears in *The Standard Edition*.

38. Ibid., 148.
39. Ibid.
40. Ibid., 151.
41. Ibid., 153.
42. Ibid., 161.
43. Ibid.
44. See Fritz Saxl, "Warburg's Visit to New Mexico" (1929/30), in *Lectures*, 1: 326. For discussion of Lippi's drawing, see Carmen C. Bambach, "Technique and Workshop Practice in Filippino's Drawings," in *The Drawings of Filippino Lippi and His Circle*, ed. George R. Goldner and Carmen C. Bambach (New York: Metropolitan Museum of Art, 1997), 26–27.
45. See Freud, *Delusions and Dreams in Jensen's "Gradiva,"* 95.
46. Sarah Kofman, *Freud and Fiction*, trans. Sarah Wykes (Cambridge: Polity Press, 1991), 113.
47. Freud, *Delusions and Dreams in Jensen's "Gradiva,"* 35.
48. Ibid., 31.
49. Ibid., 35.
50. Kofman, *Freud and Fiction*, 109.
51. Freud, *Delusions and Dreams in Jensen's "Gradiva,"* 51. Peter L. Rudnytsky explored the relationship between Freud's idea of Pompeii and his concept of therapeutic cure in his essay, "Freud's Pompeian Fantasy," in *Reading Freud's Reading*, ed. Sander L. Gilman et al. (New York: New York University Press, 1994), 213–16. Kofman discussed Hanold's cure as the result of wordplay. See Kofman, *Freud and Fiction*, 109–12.
52. Sigmund Freud, "Creative Writers and Day-Dreaming" (1908 [1907]), in *Standard Edition*, 9: 143–44.
53. Ibid., 145.
54. Ibid., 151.
55. Ibid., 152.
56. Ibid., 153.
57. Sigmund Freud, *Leonardo da Vinci and a Memory of His Childhood* (1910), in *Standard Edition*, 11: 108.
58. See Paul Ricoeur, *Freud and Philosophy: An Essay on Interpretation*, trans. Denis Savage (New Haven: Yale University Press, 1970), 173–74. Like the art historian Meyer Schapiro, the philosopher disagreed with Freud's explanation of the connections between Leonardo's life and work. Interpreting the links between the Renaissance painter's memories and his dramaturgic techniques, Ricoeur argued that "this memory only exists as a symbolizable absence . . . Leonardo's

brush does not recreate the memory of the mother, it creates it as a work of art" (ibid., 174). Schapiro's 1956 study of Freud's biography of Leonardo has been republished in Meyer Schapiro, *Theory and Philosophy of Art: Style, Artist, and Society: Selected Papers* (New York: George Braziller, 1994), 153–92. For a summary of the debate which followed the publication of Schapiro's essay, see Bradley I. Collins, *Leonardo, Psychoanalysis, and Art History: A Critical Study of Psychobiographical Approaches to Leonardo da Vinci* (Evanston, Ill.: Northwestern University Press, 1997), 44–72.

59. Freud, *Leonardo da Vinci and a Memory of His Childhood*, 69.
60. See Ernest Jones, *The Life and Work of Sigmund Freud*, vol. 2 (New York: Basic Books, 1955), 365.
61. Sigmund Freud to Martha Freud, 25 Sept. 1912, *Letters of Sigmund Freud*, 293.
62. Ricoeur, *Freud and Philosophy*, 169.
63. James Fenton, *Leonardo's Nephew: Essays on Art and Artists* (New York: Farrar, Straus and Giroux, 1998), 1.
64. Ibid., 2.
65. Sigmund Freud, "The Moses of Michelangelo" (1914), in *Standard Edition*, 13: 230.
66. Jack J. Spector suggested that Loewy's emphasis on the survival of archaic images perhaps influenced Freud's own theory of the significance of memory traces in art. See Spector, *Aesthetics of Freud*, 84–85.
67. See Sigmund Freud to Sándor Ferenczi, 23 June 1912, *The Correspondence of Sigmund Freud and Sándor Ferenczi: Volume 1, 1908–1914*, ed. Eva Brabant, Ernst Falzeder, and Patrizia Giampieri-Deutsch, under the supervision of André Haynal, trans. Peter T. Hoffer (Cambridge, Mass.: Harvard University Press, Belknap Press, 1993), 387.
68. Sigmund Freud, "The Theme of the Three Caskets" (1913), in *Standard Edition*, 12: 296.
69. Ibid., 297.
70. Ibid., 298.
71. Ibid., 299.
72. Ibid., 300.
73. Sarah Kofman emphasized the identity between Cordelia and Zoe Bertgang, and therefore also an identity between Lear and Norbert Hanold. As Kofman described, both the king and the archeologist finally resigned themselves to the fate embodied in the figures of the Graces: "Necessity for Lear to submit to death, and for Norbert to submit to life and love which are, in fact, one and the same: everyone must pay nature its dues, no-one has the right to bury himself or herself alive. Norbert is struck by madness for having attempted to transgress the laws of nature. No longer seeing or understanding anything, speaking only

dead languages, he is, before finding Zoe again, truly one of the living dead. Zoe, goddess of vegetation, worshipper of the cult of the sun, revives him. But acceptance of life is also acceptance of death when the time comes" (Kofmann, *Freud and Fiction*, 104).

74. See Hanns Sachs, "Carl Spitteler," *Imago* 2, no. 1 (1913): 73–74.

75. See Sigmund Freud, "The Dynamics of Transference" (1912), in *Standard Edition*, 12: 100 and 102.

76. See Sigmund Freud, "On the Universal Tendency to Debasement in the Sphere of Love" (1912), in *Standard Edition*, 11: 181.

77. On the relationship between reenactment and transference, see Hans W. Loewald, "Psychoanalysis as an Art and the Fantasy Character of the Psychoanalytic Situation," *Journal of the American Psychoanalytic Association* 23, no. 2 (1975): 285. The article was reprinted in Hans W. Loewald, *Papers on Psychoanalysis* (New Haven: Yale University Press, 1980). Exploring links between ancient drama and psychological science, Bennett Simon examined how the language which the ancients used in the amphitheater and in dramatic criticism also provided terminology to describe mental processes. For the connotation of stage *mimesis* as psychological identification, see Bennett Simon, *Mind and Madness in Ancient Greece: The Classical Roots of Modern Psychiatry* (Ithaca, N.Y.: Cornell University Press, 1978), 92, 97, 171.

78. Sigmund Freud, *Totem and Taboo: Some Points of Agreement between the Mental Lives of Savages and Neurotics* (1913 [1912–13]), in *Standard Edition*, 13: 91.

79. Ibid., 91n. 1.

80. Ibid., 90.

81. Ibid., 94.

82. Ibid., 134.

83. Ibid., 136.

84. René Girard, *Violence and the Sacred*, trans. Patrick Gregory (Baltimore: Johns Hopkins University Press, 1977), 219. Differing with Freud, literary scholar Girard perceived within the sons a primal mimetic desire or urge toward imitation. That desire for a model precluded any sense of rivalry and hostility originating with the son. As Girard saw, Freud's understanding of mimesis derived from his dramaturgic perspective. In Freudian theory, Girard wrote, "the little boy has no difficulty recognizing his father as a rival—a rival in the old-fashioned theatrical sense, a nuisance, a hindrance, a *terzo incommodo*" (ibid., 176). Like Girard, social psychologist Serge Moscovici argued that Freudian theory implied the existence of two fundamental and separate instincts, the erotic and mimetic. See Serge Moscovici, *The Age of the Crowd: A Historical Treatise on Mass Psychology*, trans. J. C. Whitehouse (Cambridge: Cambridge University Press, 1985), 270.

85. Freud, *Totem and Taboo*, 142.
86. Ibid., 149.

CHAPTER 4

1. E. H. Gombrich, "Sir Ernst Gombrich über seinen Lehrer Emanuel Löwy," interview by Harald Wolf, in *Emanuel Löwy: Ein vergessener Pionier*, ed. Brein, 64.
2. See Gombrich, "The Study of Art and the Study of Man: Reminiscences of Collaboration with Ernst Kris (1900–1957)," in *Tributes: Interpreters of Our Cultural Tradition* (Ithaca, N.Y.: Cornell University Press, 1984), 222, and Gombrich, *Art and Illusion*, 23, 68n, and 73.
3. Perhaps Kris's role with respect to Freud's legacy can be compared in at least one regard to Saxl's official activity. Kris helped to edit the first, abridged publication of Freud's correspondence with Wilhelm Fliess, for which he also wrote the introduction. See Ernst Kris, introduction to *The Origins of Psychoanalysis: Letters to Wilhelm Fliess*, by Sigmund Freud, ed. Marie Bonaparte, Anna Freud, and Ernst Kris, trans. Eric Mosbacher and James Strachey (New York: Basic Books, 1954, 1977), 3–45.
4. On his university registration form, however, Kris stated his religious affiliation as Roman Catholic. See *Matrikel* (Summer 1919–Summer 1922), Universitätsarchiv, Universität Wien. For Kris's background, see Elke Mühlleitner, *Biographisches Lexikon der Psychoanalyse: Die Mitglieder der Psychologischen Mittwoch-Gesellschaft und der Wiener Psychoanalytischen Vereinigung 1902–1938* (Tübingen: Edition Diskord, 1992), 187. For Saxl, see Bing, "Fritz Saxl," in *Fritz Saxl 1890–1948*, ed. Gordon, 1.
5. Max Dvořák, *The History of Art as the History of Ideas*, trans. John Hardy (London: Routledge and Kegan Paul, 1984), 26. This collection of essays was published posthumously. For Dvořák's position within the early Vienna school of art interpretation, see Christopher S. Wood, introduction to *The Vienna School Reader: Politics and Art Historical Method in the 1930s*, ed. Christopher S. Wood (New York: Zone Books, 2000), 29–31.
6. Saxl, "The Belief in Stars in the Twelfth Century" (1929/30), in *Lectures*, I: 90. For Saxl's study with Dvořák and graduation from the University of Vienna, see Bing, "Fritz Saxl," in *Fritz Saxl 1890–1948*, ed. Gordon, 2–4, and E. H. Gombrich, introduction to *A Heritage of Images: A Selection of Lectures*, by Fritz Saxl (Harmondsworth: Penguin Books, Peregrine Books, 1970), 10.
7. See Bing, "Fritz Saxl," in *Fritz Saxl 1890–1948*, ed. Gordon, 3.
8. Saxl, "Why Art History?" (1948) in *Lectures*, 1: 349.
9. Ibid., 350.

10. Ibid., 351. For a critique of Wölfflin's approach to art history by a member of the Warburg school during its Hamburg period, see Wind, "Warburg's Concept of *Kulturwissenschaft* and Its Meaning for Aesthetic Theory," in *Eloquence of Symbols*, 21–33.

11. Heinrich Wölfflin, *Principles of Art History: The Problem of the Development of Style in Later Art*, 7th ed., trans. M.D. Hottinger (New York: Dover Publications, 1950), 6.

12. Ernst Kris, "The Psychology of Caricature" (1934), in *Psychoanalytic Explorations in Art* (Madison, Conn.: International Universities Press, 1952), 177.

13. Fritz Saxl, "Macrocosm and Microcosm in Mediaeval Pictures" (1927/28), in *Lectures*, 1: 66.

14. Ginzburg, "From Aby Warburg to E. H. Gombrich: A Problem of Method," in *Clues, Myths, and the Historical Method*, 35.

15. See Mühlleitner, *Biographisches Lexikon der Psychoanalyse*, 187–88; Samuel Ritvo and Lucille B. Ritvo, "Ernst Kris, 1900–1957: Twentieth-Century *Uomo Universale*," in *Psychoanalytic Pioneers*, ed. Franz Alexander, Samuel Eisenstein, and Martin Grotjahn (New York: Basic Books, 1966), 485–89; Gombrich, "Study of Art and the Study of Man," in *Tributes*, 222–26; and Gombrich, "Sir Ernst Gombrich über seinen Lehrer Emanuel Löwy," interview by Wolf, in *Emanuel Löwy: Ein vergessener Pionier*, ed. Brein, 65.

16. The book, which was first published in 1934 under the title *Die Legende vom Künstler: Ein historischer Versuch*, appeared in English translation, with additions by Otto Kurz and a preface by E. H. Gombrich, as Ernst Kris and Otto Kurz, *Legend, Myth, and Magic in the Image of the Artist: A Historical Experiment*, trans. Alastair Lang and Lottie M. Newman (New Haven: Yale University Press, 1979). Von Schlosser's *Die Kunstliteratur: Ein Handbuch zur Quellenkunde der neueren Kunstgeschichte*, which appeared originally as a series of studies from 1914 to 1920, was published by A. Schroll of Vienna in 1924 as a single volume, for which Kris compiled the index. On Kris's work with von Schlosser, see E. H. Gombrich, preface to Kris and Kurz, *Legend, Myth, and Magic in the Image of the Artist*, ix–x.

17. Kris and Kurz, *Legend, Myth, and Magic in the Image of the Artist*, 11.

18. Ibid., 12.

19. See Sigmund Freud, "Family Romances" (1909 [1908]), in *Standard Edition*, 9: 238–41; and Otto Rank, *The Myth of the Birth of the Hero*, trans. F. Robbins and Smith Ely Jeliffe, in *The Myth of the Birth of the Hero and Other Writings*, ed. Philip Freund (New York: Random House, Vintage Books, 1959), 65–96. Freud's essay on the family romance first appeared as a section within Rank's book on hero myths, originally published in 1909.

20. Kris and Kurz, *Legend, Myth, and Magic in the Image of the Artist*, 37.

21. Ibid., 39.

22. Ibid., 66.
23. Ibid., 71.
24. As Warburg explained, the manufacture of effigies received equal support from pagan revivalists and Church officials: "By associating votive offerings with sacred images, the Catholic Church, in its wisdom, had left its formerly pagan flock a legitimate outlet for the inveterate impulse to associate oneself, or one's own effigy, with the Divine as expressed in the palpable form of a human image" (Aby Warburg, "The Art of Portraiture and the Florentine Bourgeoisie" [1902], in *Renewal of Pagan Antiquity*, 189). In Florence an outstanding example of sanctioned paganism existed in the church of Santissima Annunziata, which displayed the wax effigies of Florentine leaders. In one respect portrait art represented an extension of such effigy magic: "This lawful and persistent survival of barbarism, with wax effigies set up in church in their moldering fashionable dress, begins to cast a truer and a more favorable light on the inclusion of portrait likenesses on a church fresco of sacred scenes" (ibid., 190).
25. Kris and Kurz, *Legend, Myth, and Magic in the Image of the Artist*, 76. Recently Horst Bredekamp described how the continued fascination with automatons and their seemingly lifelike motion contributed after the Renaissance to modern reinterpretations of natural and human history. See Bredekamp, *Lure of Antiquity and the Cult of the Machine*, 46–51.
26. Kris and Kurz, *Legend, Myth, and Magic in the Image of the Artist*, 79.
27. Ibid.
28. Ibid., 93.
29. Ibid., 126.
30. Ibid., 120.
31. Ibid., 123.
32. Ibid., 132.
33. Gombrich recalled that "Kris did not want to commit Kurz, who was and remained basically a historian, beyond his chosen field. He rightly felt that he could and should expound these more technically psychoanalytic results under his own name and on his own responsibility." See Gombrich, preface to *Legend, Myth, and Magic in the Image of the Artist*, by Kris and Kurz, xiii. In the following year Kris published the paper in *Imago*.
34. Ernst Kris, "The Image of the Artist" (1935 [1934]), in *Psychoanalytic Explorations in Art*, 83.
35. Ibid.
36. Ibid.
37. Kris and Kurz, *Legend, Myth, and Magic in the Image of the Artist*, 125.
38. Jean-Pierre Vernant described the significance of masked tragedy for confronting the ancient audience with conflicting realities and meanings: "What Dionysus brought about, and what the mask also rendered possible through what was

brought to life when the actor donned it, was an eruption into the heart of public life of a dimension of existence totally alien to the quotidian world." Vernant and Frontisi-Ducroux, "Features of the Mask," 205.

39. Ernst Kris, "A Psychotic Sculptor of the Eighteenth Century" (1933 [1932]), in *Psychoanalytic Explorations in Art*, 138.

40. Ibid., 136.

41. Ibid., 137.

42. Ibid.

43. Ibid., 138. In a later essay Kris specifically cited the influence of Loewy's lecture on the protective function of art, delivered only two years before Kris wrote his essay on Messerschmidt, in shaping his own ideas on the subject. See Ernst Kris, "Approaches to Art" (1952 [1941, 1946]), in *Explorations in Art*, 50.

44. Kris, "Psychotic Sculptor of the Eighteenth Century," 138.

45. Ibid., 144.

46. Ibid.

47. Ibid.

48. Ibid., 148.

49. For a critique of Kris's formulations and an alternative reading of Messerschmidt and his work, see Rudolf Wittkower and Margot Wittkower, *Born Under Saturn: The Character and Conduct of Artists: A Documented History from Antiquity to the French Revolution* (New York: W. W. Norton, 1969), 124–132. While not rejecting the presence of mental illness, Rudolf Wittkower suggested instead that the resurgent influence of occultism in the eighteenth century or private artistic purposes unrelated to his illness more likely determined the nature of Messerschmidt's character heads. For a biographical study of Messerschmidt, with documents, see Maria Pötzl-Malikova, *Franz Xaver Messerschmidt*, Veröffentlichung der Österreichischen Galerie (Vienna: Jugend und Volk, 1982), 7–150. For the artist Arnulf Rainer's effort at reviving Messerschmidt's character heads as contemporary masks, see *Franz Xaver Messerschmidt: Character-Heads 1770–1783 Arnulf Rainer: Overdrawings Franz Xaver Messerschmidt* (London: Institute of Contemporary Arts, [1987]), 36–43. In a statement accompanying the catalog of his overdrawings, Rainer explained that "Messerschmidt's heads, like mine, have their basis in an art that is thousands of years old: that of the expressive mask." Arnulf Rainer, "My Overdrawings of Franz Xaver Messerschmidt," trans. David Britt, ibid., 35. Jill Lloyd, in her introduction to the catalog, maintained that "Messerschmidt certainly helped Rainer to discover this new landscape of the grotesque—which has the emotional intensity of insanity but also the fictive distance and self-awareness of theatre." Jill Lloyd, "Franz Xaver Messerschmidt: 'Character-Heads': Reception, Revival, Renewal," ibid., 11.

50. Kris, "The Psychology of Caricature," 179.

51. Ibid., 184.
52. Ibid., 177.
53. Gombrich, "Study of Art and the Study of Man," in *Tributes*, 227–28.
54. See E. H. Gombrich, "The Exploration of Culture Contacts: The Services to Scholarship of Otto Kurz (1908–1975)," in *Tributes*, 235–49. In the years after the war Kurz became the Warburg Institute's librarian and finally a chaired professor on its faculty.
55. See Kris and Kurz, *Die Legende vom Künstler: Ein historischer Versuch* (Wien: Krystall-Verlag, 1934), [5].
56. See E. H. Gombrich, "An Autobiographical Sketch," in *Topics of Our Time: Twentieth-Century Issues in Learning and in Art* (Berkeley and Los Angeles: University of California Press, 1991), 19–20; and Gombrich, "Study of Art and the Study of Man," in *Tributes*, 228–30. Saxl had undertaken the task of organizing for publication Warburg's private notes and materials and agreed to Gombrich serving as assistant on the project.
57. Gombrich, "Study of Art and the Study of Man," in *Tributes*, 230.
58. Ernst Kris (with E. H. Gombrich), "The Principles of Caricature" (1938 [1937]), in *Psychoanalytic Explorations in Art*, 191.
59. Ibid., 197.
60. Ibid., 199.
61. Ibid., 200.
62. Ibid., 197.
63. Ibid., 200.
64. Ibid., 201.
65. Ibid., 202.
66. Ernst Kris, "Comments on Spontaneous Artistic Creations by Psychotics" (1936), in *Psychoanalytic Explorations in Art*, 96.
67. Ibid.
68. Ibid., 98.
69. Ibid.
70. Ibid., 100.
71. Ibid., 101.
72. Ibid., 104.
73. Ibid., 103.
74. Ibid., 105.
75. Ibid., 110.
76. Ibid., 112.
77. Ibid., 113.
78. Ibid., 114.
79. Ibid., 116.

80. Ibid., 117.
81. Ernst Kris, "Ego Development and the Comic" (1938 [1937]), in *Psychoanalytic Explorations in Art*, 211.
82. Ibid.
83. Ibid., 210.
84. Ibid., 216.
85. Kris, "Approaches to Art," 39.
86. Ibid., 51–52.
87. Ibid., 56.
88. Ibid.
89. Arnold Hauser, "The Psychological Approach: Psychoanalysis and Art" (1958), in *The Philosophy of Art History* (Evanston, Ill.: Northwestern University Press, 1985), 115.
90. See Wood, introduction to *Vienna School Reader*, 12–13, 36. Julius von Schlosser, who died in the year of the *Anschluss*, himself approved of the union with Germany. See ibid., 36. Kenneth Clark recalled that following the *Anschluss* staff members of the *Kunsthistorisches Museum* who had not gone into exile greeted each other with "the obligatory 'Heil Hitler.'" See Kenneth Clark, *The Other Half: A Self-Portrait* (New York: Harper & Row, 1977), 3–4.
91. See Gombrich, "Study of Art and the Study of Man," in *Tributes*, 231–32; and Ritvo and Ritvo, "Ernst Kris, 1900–1957," in *Psychoanalytic Pioneers*, 489–92. For a memorandum to the Rockefeller Foundation in which Kris and Speier outlined their cooperative work with Kracauer, see David Culbert, "The Rockefeller Foundation, the Museum of Modern Art Film Library, and Siegfried Kracauer, 1941," *Historical Journal of Film, Radio and Television* 13, no. 4 (1993): 499–500. On the collaboration of Kris and Kracauer, see also Siegfried Kracauer to Erwin Panofsky, 1 Oct. 1941, *Siegfried Kracauer-Erwin Panofsky Briefwechsel 1941–1966*, ed. Volker Breidecker, Schriften des Warburgs-Archivs im Kunstgeschichtlichen Seminar der Universität Hamburg, Band 4 (Berlin: Akademie Verlag, 1996), 5; and Volker Breidecker, " 'Ferne Nähe': Kracauer, Panofsky und 'the Warburg tradition,'" ibid., 134, 163. After the war Kracauer appended his analysis of Nazi film propaganda to his well-known work *From Caligari to Hitler*, his study of German film during the Weimar period. See Siegfried Kracauer, *From Caligari to Hitler: A Psychological History of the German Film* (Princeton: Princeton University Press, 1947), 273–331.
92. Ernst Kris and Hans Speier, *German Radio Propaganda: Report on Home Broadcasts During the War*, in association with Sidney Axelrad, Hans Herma, Janice Loeb, Heinz Paechter, and Howard B. White (London: Oxford University Press, 1944), 36.
93. Ibid.

94. Ibid., 36–37.

95. Ibid., xi-xii.

96. Ibid., 120.

97. Ibid.

98. Ibid., 127. Democratic propaganda, Kris and Speier wrote, avoided "the tendencies that lure men toward that dream-like world where shapes replace concepts and emotions prevail over scrutiny." Ibid., 37. For Kris's comparisons of German to democratic wartime propaganda, see also his essay, "Some Problems of War Propaganda: A Note on Propaganda New and Old" (1943), in Ernst Kris, *Selected Papers of Ernst Kris*, ed. Lottie M. Newman (New Haven: Yale University Press, 1975), 445–50.

99. Ernst Kris (with Abraham Kaplan), "Aesthetic Ambiguity" (1948), in *Psychoanalytic Explorations in Art*, 243.

100. Ibid., 248.

101. Ibid.

102. Ibid., 254.

103. Ibid., 256.

104. Ibid.

105. Ibid., 258. On the contribution of Kris's theories of ambiguity and co-creation to the psychoanalytic study of art, see Ellen Handler Spitz, *Art and Psyche* (New Haven: Yale University Press, 1985), 9–10, 15–19.

106. Fritz Saxl to Aby Warburg, 14 Nov. 1916, quoted in Dorothea McEwan, " 'Mein lieber Saxl!'—'Sehr geehrter Herr Professor!': Die Aby Warburg—Fritz Saxl Korrespondenz zur Schaffung einer Forschungsbibliothek 1910 bis 1919," *Archiv für Kulturgeschichte* 80, no. 2 (1998): 431.

107. On Saxl's travels and wartime experience, see Saxl, "The History of Warburg's Library," in Gombrich, *Aby Warburg*, 328–29; Bing, "Fritz Saxl," in *Fritz Saxl 1890–1948*, ed. Gordon, 3–9; Chernow, *Warburgs*, 123–24; and McEwan, " 'Mein lieber Saxl!'—'Sehr geehrter Herr Professor!' " 430–32.

108. For Saxl's career with the Warburg Library, see Saxl, "The History of Warburg's Library," in Gombrich, *Aby Warburg*, 329–38; Bing, "Fritz Saxl," in *Fritz Saxl 1890–1948*, ed. Gordon, 9–13, 20–30, 35–37; and Chernow, *Warburgs*, 175, 206, 255–59, 262–66, 287–88, 405–8, 527.

109. Fritz Saxl, "Continuity and Variation in the Meaning of Images" (1947), in *Lectures*, 1: 2.

110. See Bing, "Fritz Saxl," in *Fritz Saxl 1890–1948*, ed. Gordon, 9.

111. For Saxl's role in preparing slides for the Kreuzlingen lecture, see Guidi, "Retracing Aby Warburg's American Journey through his Photographs," in *Photographs at the Frontier*, ed. Guidi and Mann, 33–34.

112. Fritz Saxl, "Holbein and the Reformation" (1925), in *Lectures*, I: 277.

113. Ibid., 279.
114. Ibid., 277.
115. Ibid., 279–80.
116. Ibid., 281.
117. Ibid.
118. Ibid., 284.
119. Ibid., 285.
120. Ibid. For a critique of Saxl's interpretation of the Reformation context of Holbein's work, see Ginzburg, "From Aby Warburg to E. H. Gombrich: A Problem of Method," in *Clues, Myths, and the Historical Method*, 31–34.
121. For a biographical sketch of Elsheimer, see Wittkower and Wittkower, *Born Under Saturn*, 118–20.
122. Saxl, "Elsheimer and Italy," (1930/31), in *Lectures*, 1: 290.
123. Ibid., 291.
124. Ibid., 292.
125. Ibid., 293.
126. Ibid.
127. Ibid., 296.
128. Ibid., 297.
129. Ibid.
130. Saxl, "Macrocosm and Microcosm in Mediaeval Pictures" (1927/28), in *Lectures*, 1: 66.
131. Ibid., 69.
132. Ibid., 71. Saxl's most extensive—and ultimately unfinished—collaboration with the Hamburg academic circle centered on the ancient theme of melancholy. See Raymond Klibansky, Erwin Panofsky, and Fritz Saxl, *Saturn and Melancholy: Studies in the History of Natural Philosophy, Religion, and Art* (London: Thomas Nelson and Sons, 1964), *passim*.
133. See Saul Friedländer, *Nazi Germany and the Jews*, vol. 1, *The Years of Persecution, 1933–1939* (New York: HarperCollins Publishers, Harper Perennial, 1997), 50.
134. Hugh Lloyd-Jones, "A Biographical Memoir," in Edgar Wind, *The Eloquence of Symbols: Studies in Humanist Art*, ed. Jaynie Anderson, rev. ed. (Oxford: Clarendon Press, 1993), xix. Saxl submitted his official letter of resignation to the University of Hamburg from London. See Ferretti, *Cassirer, Panofsky, and Warburg*, xv.
135. *Manchester Guardian*, 13 Dec. 1944, p. 4, quoted in Dieter Wuttke, "Die Emigration der Kulturwissenschaftlichen Bibliothek Warburg und die Anfänge des Universitätsfaches Kunstgeschichte in Großbritannien," in *Aby Warburg: Akten*, ed. Bredekamp, Diers, and Schoell-Glass, 151.
136. Fritz Saxl, "Petrarch in Venice" (1935), in *Lectures*, 1: 146.

137. Ibid., 147.
138. Fritz Saxl, "Jacopo Bellini and Mantegna as Antiquarians" (1935), in *Lectures*, 1: 157.
139. Ibid.
140. Ibid., 158.
141. Ibid., 159.
142. Saxl, "Titian and Pietro Aretino" (1935), in *Lectures*, 1: 164.
143. Ibid., 166.
144. Ibid., 169.
145. Ibid., 170.
146. Ibid., 171.
147. Ibid., 172.
148. See for example Gombrich, introduction to *Heritage of Images*, 9.
149. Fritz Saxl and Rudolf Wittkower, *British Art and the Mediterranean* (London: Geoffrey Cumberlege, Oxford University Press) first appeared in 1948, and was reprinted, with a new preface by Wittkower (London: Oxford University Press) in 1969.
150. See Fritz Saxl "Illuminated Science Manuscripts in England" (1938), in *Lectures*, 1: 105–8; "Illustrated Mediaeval Encyclopedias 1. The Classical Heritage" (1939), in *Lectures*, 1: 233–39; and "Illustrated Mediaeval Encyclopedias 2. The Christian Transformation" (1939), in *Lectures*, 1: 242–53.
151. Fritz Saxl, "Rembrandt and Classical Antiquity" (1941), in *Lectures*, 1: 310.
152. Ibid.
153. See Fritz Saxl, "Velasquez [*sic*] and Philip IV" (1942), in *Lectures*, 1: 315–18, 321–22.
154. Fritz Saxl, "The Appartamento Borgia" (1945), in *Lectures*, 1: 188.
155. In his first article for the Warburg Institute's London journal, published only months before the outbreak of war, Saxl had commented upon the ambivalent political and social nature of the rebirth of antiquity. Writing on Renaissance interest in pagan sacrificial rites, he noted that in some persons that interest reflected a renewed search for images of imperial power, while in others it even produced fevered imaginings that Jews performed the primitive practice of sacrificing humans: "people believed their neighbours to be actually offering human sacrifices, with the result that innocent people were put to death." See Fritz Saxl, "Pagan Sacrifice in the Italian Renaissance," *Journal of the Warburg Institute* 2, no. 4 (Apr. 1939): 365.
156. Fritz Saxl, "A Humanist Dreamland" (1945), in *Lectures*, 1: 226.
157. Ibid., 227.
158. Ibid., 226.
159. Saxl, "Why Art History?" (1948), in *Lectures*, 1: 355.

160. Ibid.
161. Ibid., 355–56.
162. Ibid., 356.
163. Gombrich, introduction to *Heritage of Images*, 11.

Chapter 5

1. Kenneth Clark, *Another Part of the Wood: A Self-Portrait* (New York: Harper & Row, 1974), 9.
2. Ibid., 189–90.
3. See ibid., 207–8.
4. Erik H. Erikson, *Childhood and Society*, 2d ed. (New York: W. W. Norton, 1963), 222. For Kris's early influence on Erikson, as well as his later criticisms of Erikson's theories, see Lawrence J. Friedman, *Identity's Architect: A Biography of Erik H. Erikson* (New York: Scribner, 1999), 70, 94, 239, 294; Paul Roazen, *Erik H. Erikson: The Power and Limits of a Vision* (New York: Macmillan, Free Press, 1976), 21; and Robert Coles, *Erik H. Erikson: The Growth of His Work* (Boston: Little, Brown, Atlantic Monthly Press, 1970), 23, 59, 168. On the teachings and projects of leading Viennese psychoanalysts in the 1930s, see Sheldon Gardner and Gwendolyn Stevens, *Red Vienna and the Golden Age of Psychology, 1918–1938* (New York: Praeger, 1992), 170–76, 207–38.
5. Eric Bentley, *The Life of the Drama* (New York: Atheneum, 1964; New York: Applause Theatre Books, 1991), 36.
6. Saxl, "Three 'Florentines' "(1944), in *Lectures*, 1: 335.
7. Ibid., 338.
8. Ibid., 341.
9. On Mesnil's friendship with Warburg, see Edgar Wind, "On a Recent Biography of Warburg," review of *Aby Warburg: An Intellectual Biography*, by E. H. Gombrich, in *Eloquence of Symbols*, 109. Warburg himself provided accounts of Florentine artworks to Baedeker guides. See Meyer, "Aby Warburg in His Early Correspondence," 449.
10. Saxl, "Three 'Florentines' " (1944), in *Lectures*, 1: 342.
11. Ibid.
12. Ibid.
13. Ibid.
14. Sigmund Freud, "A Disturbance of Memory on the Acropolis" (1936), in *Standard Edition*, 22: 240.
15. Ibid.
16. Ibid., 241.
17. Ibid., 244.

18. Ibid., 247–48. Ilse Grubrich-Simitis, who explored the theme of ego distur-bance in Freud's book *Moses and Monotheism*, noted that Freud was researching the book in the same time period that he wrote his letter to Rolland. See Ilse Grubrich-Simitis, *Early Freud and Late Freud: Reading Anew "Studies on Hys-teria" and "Moses and Monotheism,"* trans. Philip Slotkin (London: Routledge, 1997), 79.

Bibliography of Works Cited

Art History

Ackerman, Robert. *The Myth and Ritual School: J. G. Frazer and the Cambridge Ritualists*. New York: Garland, 1991.

Auerbach, Erich. *Mimesis: The Representation of Reality in Western Literature*. Translated by Willard R. Trask. Princeton: Princeton University Press, 1953.

Bambach, Carmen C. "Technique and Workshop Practice in Filippino's Drawings." In *The Drawings of Filippino Lippi and His Circle*, edited by George R. Goldner and Carmen C. Bambach. New York: Metropolitan Museum of Art, 1997.

Barnouw, Erik. *Documentary: A History of the Non-Fiction Film*. London: Oxford University Press, 1974.

Bazin, André. *Jean Renoir*. Edited by François Truffaut. Translated by W. W. Halsey II and William H. Simon. New York: Dell Publishing, Delta Book, 1974.

Bentley, Eric. *The Life of the Drama*. New York: Atheneum, 1964; New York: Applause Theatre Books, 1991.

Bing, Gertrud. "Fritz Saxl (1890–1948): A Memoir." In *Fritz Saxl 1890–1948: A Volume of Memorial Essays from His Friends in England*, edited by D.J. Gordon. London: Thomas Nelson and Sons, 1957.

Bredekamp, Horst. "'Du lebst und thust mir nichts': Anmerkungen zur Aktualität Aby Warburgs." In *Aby Warburg: Akten des internationalen Symposions Hamburg 1990*, edited by Horst Bredekamp, Michael Diers, and Charlotte Schoell-Glass. Weinheim: VCH, Act Humaniora, 1991.

———. *The Lure of Antiquity and the Cult of the Machine: The Kunstkammer and the Evolution of Nature, Art and Technology*. Translated by Allison Brown. Princeton: Markus Wiener, 1995.

Breidecker, Volker. "'Ferne Nähe': Kracauer, Panofsky und 'the Warburg tradition.'" In *Siegfried Kracauer-Erwin Panofsky Briefwechsel 1941–1966*, edited by Volker Breidecker. Schriften des Warburgs-Archivs im Kunstgeschichtlichen Seminar der Universität Hamburg. Band 4. Berlin: Akademie Verlag, 1996.

Brilliant, Richard. "Winckelmann and Warburg: Contrasting Attitudes toward the Instrumental Authority of Ancient Art." In *Antiquity and Its Interpreters*, edited by Alina Payne, Ann Kuttner, and Rebekah Smick. Cambridge: Cambridge University Press, 2000.

Butler, E. M. *The Tyranny of Greece over Germany: A Study of the Influence Exercised by Greek Art and Poetry over the Great German Writers of the Eighteenth, Nineteenth, and Twentieth Centuries.* Cambridge: Cambridge University Press, 1935.

Calder, William M. III, ed. *The Cambridge Ritualists Reconsidered.* Atlanta: Scholars Press, 1991.

Cassirer, Ernst. *The Philosophy of the Enlightenment.* Translated by Fritz C. A. Koelln and James B. Pettegrove. Princeton: Princeton University Press, 1951.

"Catalogue of Aby Warburg's Photographs." In *Photographs at the Frontier: Aby Warburg in America 1895–1896*, edited by Benedetta Cestelli Guidi and Nicholas Mann. London: Merrell Holberton, The Warburg Institute, 1998.

Chernow, Ron. *The Warburgs: The Twentieth-Century Odyssey of a Remarkable Jewish Family.* New York: Random House, 1993.

Clark, Kenneth. *Another Part of the Wood: A Self-Portrait.* New York: Harper & Row, 1974.

———. *The Other Half: A Self-Portrait.* New York: Harper & Row, 1977.

Collins, Bradley I. *Leonardo, Psychoanalysis, and Art History: A Critical Study of Psychobiographical Approaches to Leonardo da Vinci.* Evanston, Ill.: Northwestern University Press, 1997.

Cornford, Francis M. *Thucydides Mythistoricus.* Philadelphia: University of Pennsylvania Press, 1971.

Culbert, David. "The Rockefeller Foundation, the Museum of Modern Art Film Library, and Siegfried Kracauer, 1941." *Historical Journal of Film, Radio and Television* 13, no. 4 (1993): 495–511.

Cuzin, Jean-Pierre. *Raphael: His Life and Works.* Translated by Sarah Brown. Secaucus, N.J.: Chartwell Books, 1985.

Dvořák, Max. *The History of Art as the History of Ideas.* Translated by John Hardy. London: Routledge & Kegan Paul, 1984.

Else, Gerald F. *The Origin and Early Form of Greek Tragedy.* New York: W. W. Norton, 1972.

Farrer, David. *The Warburgs: The Story of a Family.* New York: Stein and Day, 1974.

Fenton, James. *Leonardo's Nephew: Essays on Art and Artists.* New York: Farrar, Straus and Giroux, 1998.

Ferretti, Silvia. *Cassirer, Panofsky, and Warburg: Symbol, Art, and History.* Translated by Richard Pierce. New Haven: Yale University Press, 1989.

Finley, M. I. "Anthropology and the Classics" (1972). In *The Use and Abuse of History.* London: Penguin Books, 1990.

Forster, Kurt W. "Aby Warburg: His Study of Ritual and Art on Two Continents." *October* 77 (Summer 1996): 5–24.

———. Introduction to *The Renewal of Pagan Antiquity: Contributions to the Cultural History of the European Renaissance*, by Aby Warburg. Los Angeles: Getty Research Institute for the History of Art and the Humanities, 1999.

Geertz, Armin W. "Pueblo Cultural History." In *Photographs at the Frontier: Aby Warburg in America, 1895–1896*, edited by Benedetta Cestelli Guidi and Nicholas Mann. London: Merrell Holberton, The Warburg Institute, 1998.

Gilbert, Felix. "From Art History to the History of Civilization: Aby Warburg" (1972). Review of *Aby Warburg: An Intellectual Biography*, by E. H. Gombrich. In *History: Choice and Commitment.* Cambridge, Mass.: Harvard University Press, Belknap Press, 1977.

Ginzburg, Carlo. "From Aby Warburg to E. H. Gombrich: A Problem of Method." In *Clues, Myth, and the Historical Method.* Translated by John and Anne Tedeschi. Baltimore: Johns Hopkins University Press, 1989.

Gombrich, E. H. *Aby Warburg: An Intellectual Biography.* 2d ed. Chicago: University of Chicago Press, 1986.

———. *Art and Illusion: A Study in the Psychology of Pictorial Representation.* The A. W. Mellon Lectures in the Fine Arts, 1956. Bollingen Series. Princeton: Princeton University Press, 1969.

———. "An Autobiographical Sketch." In *Topics of Our Time: Twentieth-Century Issues in Learning and in Art.* Berkeley and Los Angeles: University of California Press, 1991.

———. "The Exploration of Culture Contacts: The Services to Scholarship of Otto Kurz (1908–1975)." In *Tributes: Interpreters of Our Cultural Tradition.* Ithaca, N.Y.: Cornell University Press, 1984.

———. Introduction to *A Heritage of Images*, by Fritz Saxl. Harmondsworth: Penguin Books, Peregrine Books, 1970.

———. Preface to *Legend, Myth, and Magic in the Image of the Artist: A Historical Experiment*, by Ernst Kris and Otto Kurz. New Haven: Yale University Press, 1979.

———. "Raphael's *Stanza della Segnatura* and the Nature of its Symbolism." In *Symbolic Images*, 3d ed. London: Phaidon Press, 1985.

———. "Sir Ernst Gombrich über seinen Lehrer Emanuel Löwy." Interview by Harald Wolf. In *Emanuel Löwy: Ein vergessener Pionier*, edited by Friedrich Brein. Kataloge der Archäologischen Sammlung der Universität Wien. Sonderheft 1. Vienna: Verlag des Clubs der Universität Wien, 1998.

———. "The Study of Art and the Study of Man: Reminiscences of Collaboration with Ernst Kris (1900–1957)." In *Tributes: Interpreters of Our Cultural Tradition.* Ithaca, N.Y.: Cornell University Press, 1984.

Guidi, Benedetta Cestelli. "Retracing Aby Warburg's American Journey through his Photographs." In *Photographs at the Frontier: Aby Warburg in America, 1895–1896*, edited by Benedetta Cestelli Guidi and Nicholas Mann. London: Merrell Holberton, The Warburg Institute, 1998.

Harrison, Jane Ellen. *Ancient Art and Ritual.* New York: Henry Holt, 1913.

Hauser, Arnold. "The Psychological Approach: Psychoanalysis and Art" (1958). In *The Philosophy of Art History.* Evanston, Ill.: Northwestern University Press, 1985.

———. *The Social History of Art.* Vol. 1, *Prehistoric Times, Ancient-Oriental Urban Cultures, Greece and Rome, The Middle Ages.* New York: Vintage Books, 1951.

Hoffmann, Konrad. "Angst und Methode nach Warburg: Erinnerung als Veränderung." In *Aby Warburg: Akten des internationalen Symposions Hamburg 1990*, edited by Horst Bredekamp, Michael Diers, and Charlotte Schoell-Glass. Weinheim: VCH, Act Humaniora, 1991.

Holly, Michael Ann. *Panofsky and the Foundations of Art History.* Ithaca, N.Y.: Cornell University Press, 1984.

Hollander, Anne. *Moving Pictures.* Cambridge, Mass.: Harvard University Press, 1991.

Iversen, Margaret. "Retrieving Warburg's Tradition." *Art History* 16, no. 4 (Dec. 1993): 541–53.

Jensen, Wilhelm. "Gradiva: A Pompeiian Fancy." Translated by Helen M. Downey. In Sigmund Freud, *Delusion and Dream and Other Essays*, edited by Philip Rieff. Boston: Beacon Press, 1956.

Klibansky, Raymond, Erwin Panofsky, and Fritz Saxl. *Saturn and Melancholy: Studies in the History of Natural Philosophy, Religion, and Art.* London: Thomas Nelson and Sons, 1964.

Kracauer, Siegfried. *From Caligari to Hitler: A Psychological History of the German Film.* Princeton: Princeton University Press, 1947.

Lecoq, Jacques. "Theatre of Gesture and Image." Translated by Shelley Tepperman. In *The Intercultural Performance Reader*, edited by Patrice Pavis. London: Routledge, 1996.

Lee, Rensselaer W. *Ut Pictura Poesis: The Humanistic Theory of Painting.* New York: W. W. Norton, 1967.

Lessing, Gotthold Ephraim. *Laocoon or On the Limits of Painting and Poetry* (1766). Translated by William A. Steel and revised by H. B. Nisbet. In *German Aesthetic and Literary Criticism: Winckelmann, Lessing, Hamann, Herder, Schiller, Goethe*, edited by H. B. Nisbet. Cambridge: Cambridge University Press, 1985.

———. *Nathan the Wise* (1779). Translated by William A. Steel. In *Laocoön, Nathan the Wise, Minna von Barnhelm.* Edited by William A. Steel. London: J. M. Dent and Sons, 1930, 1961.

Levi, Primo. "Renzo's Fist." In *Other People's Trades.* Translated by Raymond Rosenthal. London: Abacus, 1991.

Lloyd, Jill. "Franz Xaver Messerschmidt: 'Character-Heads': Reception, Revival,

Renewal." In *Franz Xaver Messerschmidt: Character-Heads 1770–1783 Arnulf Rainer: Overdrawings Franz Xaver Messerschmidt.* London: Institute of Contemporary Arts, [1987].

Lloyd-Jones, Hugh. "A Biographical Memoir." In Edgar Wind, *The Eloquence of Symbols: Studies in Humanist Art,* edited by Jaynie Anderson. Rev. ed. Oxford: Clarendon Press, 1993.

Loewy, Emanuel. *The Rendering of Nature in Early Greek Art.* Translated by John Fothergill. London: Duckworth and Co., 1907.

———."Ursprünge der bildenden Kunst." *Almanach der Akademie der Wissenschaften in Wien* 80 (1930): 275–95.

McEwan, Dorothea. " 'Mein lieber Saxl!'—'Sehr geehrter Herr Professor!': Die Aby Warburg—Fritz Saxl Korrespondenz zur Schaffung einer Forschungsbibliothek 1910 bis 1919," *Archiv für Kulturgeschichte* 80, no. 2 (1998): 417–33.

Meyer, A. M. "Aby Warburg in His Early Correspondence." *American Scholar* 57 (Summer 1988): 445–52.

Michaud, Philippe-Alain. *Aby Warburg et l'image en mouvement.* Paris: Éditions Macula, 1998.

———. "Florence in New Mexico: The Intermezzi of 1589 in the Light of Indian Rituals." In *Photographs at the Frontier: Aby Warburg in America 1895–1896*, edited by Benedetta Cestelli Guidi and Nicholas Mann. London: Merrell Holberton, The Warburg Institute, 1998.

Momigliano, Arnaldo. "Jacob Bernays" (1969). In *A. D. Momigliano: Studies on Modern Scholarship*, edited by G. W. Bowersock and T. J. Cornell. Translated by T. J. Cornell. Berkeley and Los Angeles: University of California Press, 1994.

Pötzl-Malikova, Maria. *Franz Xaver Messerschmidt.* Veröffentlichung der Österreichischen Galerie. Vienna: Jugend und Volk, 1982.

Rainer, Arnulf. "My Overdrawings of Franz Xaver Messerschmidt." Translated by David Britt. In *Franz Xaver Messerschmidt: Character-Heads 1770–1783 Arnulf Rainer: Overdrawings Franz Xaver Messerschmidt.* London: Institute of Contemporary Arts, [1987].

Rampley, Matthew. "From Symbol to Allegory: Aby Warburg's Theory of Art." *Art Bulletin* 79, no. 1 (Mar. 1997): 41–55.

Renoir, Jean. *An Interview.* København, Denmark: Green Integer Books, 1998.

———. *My Life and My Films.* Translated by Norman Denny. New York: Atheneum, 1974.

———. *Renoir, My Father.* Translated by Randolph and Dorothy Weaver. Boston: Little, Brown, 1958.

Robertson, Ritchie. *The 'Jewish Question' in German Literature 1749–1939: Emancipation and Its Discontents.* Oxford: Oxford University Press, 1999.

Roeck, Bernd. "Psychohistorie im Zeichen Saturns: Aby Warburgs Denksystem und die moderne Kulturgeschichte." In *Kulturgeschichte Heute*, edited by Wolfgang

Hardtwig and Hans-Ulrich Wehler. Göttingen: Vandenhoeck & Ruprecht, 1996.

Saxl, Fritz. "The Classical Inscription in Renaissance Art and Politics." *Journal of the Warburg and Courtauld Institutes* 4, no. 1 and 2 (Oct.-Jan. 1940–41): 19–42.

———. *A Heritage of Images: A Selection of Lectures.* Edited by Hugh Honour and John Fleming. Harmondsworth: Penguin Books, Peregrine Books, 1970.

———. "The History of Warburg's Library (1886–1944)." In E. H. Gombrich, *Aby Warburg: An Intellectual Biography*, 2d ed. Chicago: University of Chicago Press, 1986.

———. *Lectures.* 2 vols. London: The Warburg Institute, University of London, 1957.

———. "Pagan Sacrifice in the Italian Renaissance." *Journal of the Warburg Institute* 2, no. 4 (Apr. 1939): 346–67.

Saxl, Fritz, and Rudolf Wittkower. *British Art and the Mediterranean.* London: Geoffrey Cumberlege, Oxford University Press, 1948. Reprint, with a preface by Rudolf Wittkower, London: Oxford University Press, 1969.

Schade, Sigrid. "Charcot and the Spectacle of the Hysterical Body: The 'Pathos Formula' as an Aesthetic Staging of Psychiatric Discourse—a Blind Spot in the Reception of Warburg." *Art History* 18, no. 4 (Dec. 1995): 499–517.

Schapiro, Meyer. *Theory and Philosophy of Art: Style, Artist, and Society: Selected Papers.* New York: George Braziller, 1994.

Schlosser, Julius von. *Die Kunstliteratur: Ein Handbuch zur Quellenkunde der neueren Kunstgeschichte.* Vienna: A. Schroll, 1924.

Schoell-Glass, Charlotte. *Aby Warburg und der Antisemitismus: Kulturwissenschaft als Geistespolitik.* Frankfurt am Main: Fischer Taschenbuch Verlag, 1998.

Sesonske, Alexander. *Jean Renoir: The French Films, 1924–1939.* Harvard Film Studies. Cambridge, Mass.: Harvard University Press, 1980.

Settis, Salvatore. "Kunstgeschichte als vergleichende Kulturwissenschaft: Aby Warburg, die Pueblo-Indianer und das Nachleben der Antike." In *Künstlerischer Austausch Artistic Exchange: Akten des XXVIII. Internationalen Kongresses für Kunstgeschichte*, edited by Thomas W. Gaehtgens. Vol. 1. Berlin: Akademie Verlag, 1993.

Siegfried Kracauer-Erwin Panofsky Briefwechsel 1941–1966. Edited by Volker Breidecker. Schriften des Warburgs-Archivs im Kunstgeschichtlichen Seminar der Universität Hamburg. Band 4. Berlin: Akademie Verlag, 1996.

Steinberg, Michael P. "Aby Warburg's Kreuzlingen Lecture: A Reading." In *Images from the Region of the Pueblo Indians of North America*, by Aby Warburg. Ithaca, N.Y.: Cornell University Press, 1995.

Vernant, Jean-Pierre. "The Birth of Images." Translated by Froma I. Zeitlin. In *Mortals and Immortals: Collected Essays.* Edited by Froma I. Zeitlin. Princeton: Princeton University Press, 1991.

———. "The Tragic Subject: Historicity and Transhistoricity." In Jean-Pierre Vernant and Pierre Vidal-Naquet, *Myth and Tragedy in Ancient Greece.* Translated by Janet Lloyd. New York: Zone Books, 1990.

Vernant, Jean-Pierre, and Françoise Frontisi-Ducroux. "Features of the Mask in Ancient Greece." In Jean-Pierre Vernant and Pierre Vidal-Naquet, *Myth and Tragedy in Ancient Greece.* Translated by Janet Lloyd. New York: Zone Books, 1990.

Warburg, Aby. *Images from the Region of the Pueblo Indians of North America.* Translated by Michael P. Steinberg. Ithaca, N.Y.: Cornell University Press, 1995.

———. *The Renewal of Pagan Antiquity: Contributions to the Cultural History of the European Renaissance.* Translated by David Britt. Getty Research Institute Publications Programs: Texts and Documents. Los Angeles: Getty Research Institute for the History of Art and the Humanities, 1999.

Wind, Edgar. "On a Recent Biography of Warburg" (1971). Review of *Aby Warburg: An Intellectual Biography*, by E. H. Gombrich. In *The Eloquence of Symbols: Studies in Humanist Art*, edited by Jaynie Anderson. Rev. ed. Oxford: Clarendon Press, 1993.

———. "Warburg's Concept of *Kulturwissenschaft* and its Meaning for Aesthetics" (1930). In *The Eloquence of Symbols: Studies in Humanist Art*, edited by Jaynie Anderson. Rev. ed. Oxford: Clarendon Press, 1993.

Wittkower, Rudolf, and Margot Wittkower. *Born Under Saturn: The Character and Conduct of Artists: A Documented History from Antiquity to the French Revolution.* New York: W. W. Norton, 1969.

Wolf, Harald. "Emanuel Löwy: Leben und Werk eines vergessenen Pioniers." In *Emanuel Löwy: Ein vergessener Pionier*, edited by Friedrich Brien. Kataloge der Archäologischen Sammlung der Universität Wien. Sonderheft 1. Vienna: Verlag des Clubs der Universität Wien, 1998.

Wölfflin, Heinrich. *Principles of Art History: The Problem of the Development of Style in Later Art.* 7th ed. Translated by M. D. Hottinger. New York: Dover Publications, 1950.

Wood, Christopher S. Introduction to *The Vienna School Reader: Politics and Art Historical Method in the 1930s*, edited by Christopher S. Wood. New York: Zone Books, 2000.

Wuttke, Dieter. "Die Emigration der Kulturwissenschaftlichen Bibliothek Warburg und die Anfänge des Universitätsfaches Kunstgeschichte in Großbritannien." In *Aby Warburg: Akten des internationalen Symposions Hamburg 1990*, edited by Horst Bredekamp, Michael Diers, and Charlotte Schoell-Glass. Weinheim: VCH, Act Humaniora, 1991.

Sigmund Freud

The Standard Edition of the Complete Psychological Works of Sigmund Freud. 24 vols. Edited by James Strachey in collaboration with Anna Freud, assisted by Alix Strachey and Alan Tyson. London: Hogarth Press and the Institute of Psycho-Analysis, 1953–74.

The Interpretation of Dreams (1900). Vols. 4–5.

Jokes and their Relation to the Unconscious (1905). Vol. 8.

Delusions and Dreams in Jensen's "Gradiva" (1907 [1906]). Vol. 9.

"Creative Writers and Day-Dreaming" (1908 [1907]). Vol. 9.

"Family Romances" (1909 [1908]). Vol. 9.

Leonardo da Vinci and a Memory of His Childhood (1910). Vol. 11.

"On the Universal Tendency to Debasement in the Sphere of Love" (1912). Vol. 11.

"The Dynamics of Transference" (1912). Vol. 12.

"The Theme of the Three Caskets" (1913). Vol. 12.

Totem and Taboo: Some Points of Agreement between the Mental Lives of Savages and Neurotics (1913 [1912–13]). Vol. 13.

"The Moses of Michelangelo" (1914). Vol. 13.

Civilization and Its Discontents (1930 [1929]). Vol. 21.

"A Disturbance of Memory on the Acropolis" (1936). Vol. 22.

Moses and Monotheism: Three Essays (1939 [1934–38]). Vol. 23.

Psychoanalysis

Adams, Laurie Schneider. *Art and Psychoanalysis.* New York: HarperCollins Publishers, Icon Editions, 1993.

Coles, Robert. *Erik H. Erikson: The Growth of His Work.* Boston: Little, Brown, Atlantic Monthly Press, 1970.

The Complete Letters of Sigmund Freud to Wilhelm Fliess 1887–1904. Edited and translated by Jeffrey Moussaieff Masson. Cambridge, Mass.: Harvard University Press, Belknap Press, 1985.

The Correspondence of Sigmund Freud and Sándor Ferenczi: Volume 1, 1908–1914. Edited by Eva Brabant, Ernst Falzeder, and Patrizia Giampieri-Deutsch, under the supervision of André Haynal. Translated by Peter T. Hoffer. Cambridge, Mass.: Harvard University Press, Belknap Press, 1993.

Erikson, Erik H. *Childhood and Society.* 2d ed. New York: W. W. Norton, 1963.

Frankland, Graham. *Freud's Literary Culture.* Cambridge: Cambridge University Press, 2000.

Freud, Sigmund. *The Origins of Psychoanalysis: Letters to Wilhelm Fliess.* Edited by Marie

Bonaparte, Anna Freud, and Ernst Kris. Translated by Eric Mosbacher and James Strachey. New York: Basic Books, 1954, 1977.

Friedländer, Saul. *History and Psychoanalysis: An Inquiry into the Possibilities and Limits of Psychohistory*. Translated by Susan Suleiman. New York: Holmes and Meier, 1978.

———. *Nazi Germany and the Jews*. Vol. 1: *The Years of Persecution, 1933–1939*. New York: HarperCollins Publishers, Harper Perennial, 1997.

Friedman, Lawrence J. *Identity's Architect: A Biography of Erik H. Erikson*. New York: Scribner, 1999.

Gardner, Sheldon, and Gwendolyn Stevens. *Red Vienna and the Golden Age of Psychology, 1918–1938*. New York: Praeger, 1992.

Girard, René. *Violence and the Sacred*. Translated by Patrick Gregory. Baltimore: Johns Hopkins University Press, 1977.

Grubrich-Simitis, Ilse. *Early Freud and Late Freud: Reading Anew "Studies on Hysteria" and "Moses and Monotheism"*. Translated by Philip Slotkin. London: Routledge, 1997.

Jones, Ernest. *The Life and Work of Sigmund Freud*, 3 vols. New York: Basic Books, 1953–57.

Kofman, Sarah. *Freud and Fiction*. Translated by Sarah Wykes. Cambridge, Mass.: Polity Press, 1991.

Kraus, Karl. *Die Fackel* 9, no. 229 (2 July 1907).

Kris, Ernst. *Psychoanalytic Explorations in Art*. Madison, Conn.: International Universities Press, 1952.

———. "Some Problems of War Propaganda: A Note on Propaganda New and Old" (1943). In *Selected Papers of Ernst Kris*, edited by Lottie M. Newman. New Haven: Yale University Press, 1975.

———. Introduction to *The Origins of Psychoanalysis: Letters to Wilhelm Fliess*, by Sigmund Freud. Edited by Marie Bonaparte, Anna Freud, and Ernst Kris. Translated by Eric Mosbacher and James Strachey. New York: Basic Books, 1954, 1977.

Kris, Ernst, and Otto Kurz. *Die Legende vom Künstler: Ein geschichtlicher Versuch*. Wien: Krystall-Verlag, 1934.

———. *Legend, Myth, and Magic in the Image of the Artist: A Historical Experiment*. Translated by Alastair Laing and revised by Lottie M. Newman. New Haven: Yale University Press, 1979.

Kris, Ernst, and Hans Speier. *German Radio Propaganda: Report on Home Broadcasts During the War*. In association with Sidney Axelrad, Hans Herma, Janice Loeb, Heinz Paechter, and Howard B. White. Studies of the Institute of World Affairs. London: Oxford University Press, 1944.

The Letters of Sigmund Freud. Edited by Ernst L. Freud. Translated by Tania and James

Stern. New York: Basic Books, 1960.

The Letters of Sigmund Freud and Arnold Zweig. Edited by Ernst L. Freud. Translated by Elaine and William Robson-Scott. New York: Harcourt Brace Jovanovich, Helen and Kurt Wolff Book, 1970.

Loewald, Hans W. "Psychoanalysis as an Art and the Fantasy Character of the Psychoanalytic Situation." *Journal of the American Psychoanalytic Association* 23, no. 2 (1975): 277–99. Reprinted in Hans W. Loewald, *Papers on Psychoanalysis.* New Haven: Yale University Press, 1980.

Lyotard, Jean-François. "The Unconscious as Mise-en-Scène" (1977). Translated by Joseph Maier. In *Mimesis, Masochism, and Mime: The Politics of Theatricality in Contemporary French Thought,* edited by Timothy Murray. Ann Arbor: University of Michigan Press, 1997.

Matrikel (Summer 1919–Summer 1922). Universitätsarchiv, Universität Wien.

Moscovici, Serge. *The Age of the Crowd: A Historical Treatise on Mass Psychology.* Translated by J. C. Whitehouse. Cambridge: Cambridge University Press, 1985.

Mühlleitner, Elke. *Biographisches Lexikon der Psychoanalyse: Die Mitglieder der Psychologischen Mittwoch-Gesellschaft und der Wiener Psychoanalytischen Vereinigung 1902–1938.* Tübingen: Edition Diskord, 1992.

Rank, Otto. *The Myth of the Birth of the Hero.* Translated by F. Robbins and Smith Ely Jeliffe. In *The Myth of the Birth of the Hero and Other Writings,* edited by Philip Freund. New York: Random House, Vintage Books, 1959.

Ricoeur, Paul. *Freud and Philosophy: An Essay on Interpretation.* Translated by Denis Savage. New Haven: Yale University Press, 1970.

Ritvo, Samuel, and Lucille B. Ritvo. "Ernst Kris 1900–1957: Twentieth-Century *Uomo Universale.*" In *Psychoanalytic Pioneers,* edited by Franz Alexander, Samuel Eisenstein, and Martin Grotjahn. New York: Basic Books, 1966.

Roazen, Paul. *Erik H. Erikson: The Power and Limits of a Vision.* New York: Macmillan, Free Press, 1976.

Rose, Louis. *The Freudian Calling: Early Viennese Psychoanalysis and the Pursuit of Cultural Science.* Detroit: Wayne State University Press, 1998.

Rudnytsky, Peter L. "Freud's Pompeian Fantasy." In *Reading Freud's Reading,* edited by Sander L. Gilman et al. New York: New York University Press, 1994

Sachs, Hanns. "Carl Spitteler." *Imago* 2, no. 1 (1913): 73–77.

Schönau, Walter. *Sigmund Freuds Prosa: Literarische Elemente seines Stils.* Stuttgart: J. B. Metzlersche Verlagsbuchhandlung, 1968.

Schorske, Carl E. "To the Egyptian Dig: Freud's Psycho-Archeology of Cultures." In *Thinking With History: Explorations in the Passage to Modernism.* Princeton: Princeton University Press, 1998.

Simon, Bennett. *Mind and Madness in Ancient Greece: The Classical Roots of Modern Psychiatry.* Ithaca, N.Y.: Cornell University Press, 1978.

Bibliography

Spector, Jack J. *The Aesthetics of Freud: A Study in Psychoanalysis and Art.* New York: McGraw-Hill, 1974.

Spitz, Ellen Handler. *Art and Psyche: A Study in Psychoanalysis and Aesthetics,* New Haven: Yale University Press, 1985.

Wortis, Joseph. *Fragments of an Analysis with Freud.* New York: McGraw-Hill, 1975.

Yerushalmi, Yosef Hayim. *Freud's Moses: Judaism Terminable and Interminable.* New Haven: Yale University Press, 1991.

Index